where you

left me

where you
left me

A MEMOIR

Jennifer Gardner Trulson

GALLERY BOOKS

New York · London · Toronto · Sydney · New Delhi

Certain names and identifying characteristics have been changed.

Gallery Books
A Division of Simon & Schuster, Inc.
1230 Avenue of the Americas
New York, NY 10020

Copyright © 2011 by Jennifer Gardner Trulson

"Songbird": Words and Music by Christine McVie
Copyright © 1977 by Universal Music–Careers
Copyright Renewed
International Copyright Secured. All Rights Reserved.
Reprinted by permission of Hal Leonard Corporation

First Gallery Books hardcover edition August 2011

GALLERY BOOKS and colophon are registered trademarks of Simon & Schuster, Inc.

For information about special discounts for bulk purchases, please contact Simon & Schuster Special Sales at 1-866-506-1949 or business@ simonandschuster.com

The Simon & Schuster Speakers Bureau can bring authors to your live event. For more information or to book an event contact the Simon & Schuster Speakers Bureau at 1-866-248-3049 or visit our website at www.simonspeakers.com.

Designed by Jaime Putorti

Manufactured in the United States of America

10   9   8   7   6   5   4   3   2   1

Library of Congress Cataloging-in-Publication Data is available.

ISBN 978-1-4516-2142-6
ISBN 978-1-4516-2144-0 (ebook)

For Derek,
who gave me a second chance
to fall in love for the first time.

For Julia and Michael,
who kept us afloat and continue
to astonish me.

1

———————

"It's coming down," I said to myself as I blearily looked out my office window on the thirtieth floor at 1585 Broadway. The snowstorm had picked up, and Times Square slept under a deep cover of untouched snow. It was a rare sight, even at 1:00 a.m.—not a car or pedestrian to be seen for blocks under the blazing neon lights and billboards. I was used to working late, churning out contracts, memos, and research day and night as a third-year associate at a law firm. And normally, I'd take a town car home at this hour, but not even taxis were out in this weather—nothing had been plowed and the sidewalks were piled high with four-foot drifts of snow. How the hell was I going to get home? Walking wasn't an option, I lived all the way across town on First Avenue. The subway was running, but I wasn't about to take a train home alone from Times Square at one in the morning.

I went back up to my office and nervously called Doug. Doug and I had been seeing each other steadily since our first date at

Café Luxembourg four months earlier. It was a blind date, my third one that week. My job didn't afford me much time for a proper social life, leaving me at the mercy of my friends to make introductions. At first, I wasn't sure Doug could be the one for me. Yes, he was handsome—six foot four with clear blue eyes, a radiant smile, and the large build of a professional quarterback. It took me two dates to realize that he had a small bald spot on the top of his head because he towered over me by nearly a foot. He was also fiercely intelligent and attentive, but I worried that he might be a little too reserved and formal. Doug was born and raised in Manhattan, a true city boy who relished the pace of his hometown and seemed to know everyone. I grew up in Longmeadow, a small town in Massachusetts, and had only moved to the city two years prior after graduating from Harvard Law School. I hardly knew anyone, but I loved New York—the frenetic energy, crowded sidewalks, and diverse neighborhoods sang to me.

I was further thrown by my realization that Doug was also a grown-up, a creature I had never dated before. He was five years older than I, took me to popular restaurants and cultural events around the city, and he always paid, dropped me off at my door, and called the next day. This gallant behavior confused me. I was used to meeting dates at neighborhood dives and splitting the check.

For weeks, he courted me in his old-fashioned manner, and I vacillated between being attracted to him and questioning whether I really wanted to continue the relationship. I was twenty-seven years old, what did I know? Doug, however, had what I liked to call a healthy self-image and watched me with great amusement while I turned myself into a pretzel trying to figure out where we stood. One night in October, while standing in line to see *The Age of Innocence*, I casually remarked that, maybe, I liked him only "as a friend," and that we should leave it at that. He lifted my chin with his hand and said confidently, "I'm not worried about you. You'll smarten up."

⋯⋯

Doug answered the phone in his loft on West Fifteenth Street with a sleepy "Hello?" I apologized for waking him and asked if he could convince one of his company's car services to send a car to take me home. Doug was a senior executive at Cantor Fitzgerald, an international brokerage firm run by his best friend from college, Howard Lutnick. Apart from a few years at Lehman Brothers right after graduating from Haverford College, Doug had spent the better part of the last decade working with his father in the family real estate development and management business. But as the housing market softened in the early nineties, he was ready for a new challenge when Howard offered him the position and Doug gladly accepted.

When I called that night, Doug told me to wait in the lobby—he was coming to get me himself—then hung up before I could stop him. Twenty minutes later, as I stood in the empty lobby in my impractical heels, watching the wind whip clouds of snow around the dark, deserted streets, I saw his large frame lumbering through the snowy drifts to my building. Poorly dressed for the weather, Doug's wide-open parka flapped in the wind, and one leg of his sweatpants was tucked into his Timberlands while the other hung loose at his ankle. When he arrived at the door, Doug's bare head and shoulders were covered in snowflakes, and his round glasses were dripping wet. "Come with me," my disheveled knight said with a breathless smile. He reached out his hand and carried me through the snow, into the subway and home to safety.

September 10, 2001

Doug's fortieth birthday was coming up and I decided to surprise him with a Studio 54–themed party—vintage costumes, psychedelic décor, and all the Bee Gees music one could stand. Doug had an unnatural attachment to this era—he often ordered double-disc sets of seventies hits from late-night infomercials. The party was scheduled for the first Saturday of October, and I mailed the invitations that afternoon; the front of the colorful card said "Burn, Baby, Burn."

That evening, Doug met me on West Sixty-Eighth Street at our children's preschool, Stephen Wise Synagogue, for parent orientation. The next day, Tuesday the eleventh, Michael, our four-year-old, would have his first day of prekindergarten. Julia, our two-and-a-half-year-old, would start preschool for the first time on Wednesday. I was already sitting in a child-size wooden chair in Michael's classroom with the other parents in a semicircle when Doug's face appeared in the doorway. His bright blue eyes found mine, and he carefully navigated through the crowded classroom to join me. It didn't matter how long we'd been together, my heart literally jumped whenever he entered a room. All of the chairs were taken; I slid to the floor so that my tall husband could sit. "Hi, Bunny," he whispered in my ear as I settled against his legs. While the teacher spoke, Doug unconsciously stroked my hair as he always did and valiantly tried to sit patiently, folded up like a grizzly bear in a baby's car seat. We took turns visiting each child's classroom and placed good luck notes in Michael's and Julia's cubbies.

When orientation ended, Doug's glance told me that he wanted to get right home to the kids before their bedtimes; no parent-to-parent small talk. Doug and I had nearly perfected the art of private marital communication in public places. A raised eyebrow, a tickle on the back of my arm, or a well-timed kiss on the cheek would signal, "Wrap it up, I want you to myself." On the rare occasion I missed one of his signs or continued to embed myself in conversation, he'd raise the stakes and call me Abby, as in, "Abby, you look lovely tonight." Abby stood for "oblivious," and it was Doug's covert way of telling me to stop talking. I stopped. Immediately. What wife wouldn't happily oblige a husband who couldn't wait to steal any moment he could to be alone with her?

On the morning of September 11, the alarm buzzed at 5:30 a.m., and Doug lurched out of bed to meet his trainer at our gym. I went back to sleep and woke an hour later to his big, scratchy face rubbing against my cheek. "Wake up, beautiful." He always woke me this way, unless Michael had already scampered under the covers for a morning snuggle. After Doug showered, I followed him to our small office down the hall where he kept his work clothes. I sat at the desk in my bathrobe while he got dressed—loafers, khaki trousers, a brown leather belt. He was particularly delighted to show me the new blue oxford shirt he'd bought the day before at Rothmans in Union Square. "See, I picked it out myself," he proudly said as he turned from side to side, playfully modeling for me. "I'm very impressed, Grasshopper," I replied, taking note of this historic moment. Doug hated shopping and could wear his clothes until they were threadbare and tragically out of style. Ever since we'd gotten married, he'd gratefully assigned me the task of dressing him and rarely bought anything on his own.

Today was going to be special. It was Michael's first day of school and Doug's father's seventy-second birthday; we planned to take the kids for the first time to dinner at a "grown-up" restaurant, Shun Lee, to celebrate with the grandparents. Doug couldn't take Michael to school since he had scheduled early meetings at the office that he wanted to handle in order to keep our five-o'clock dinner reservation. Ironically, Doug was supposed to have been traveling that day, but postponed the trip to celebrate his dad's birthday and mark Julia's first day of preschool on the twelfth.

I actually ribbed Doug a little for not accompanying us to school that morning. "You'll miss Michael's first-day pictures. He'll remember this." Doug gave me his usual bemused I'm-the-best-thing-that-ever-happened-to-you look and told me not to kvetch. Honestly, I wasn't upset at all. Doug never really irritated me. Occasionally we'd bicker or roll our eyes at each other, but no argument ever escalated into a bitter exchange. Doug was my hero. It sounds pat—as if I'm sanctifying him—but it's the truth. He specifically promised me three things before we got married: he promised he would always "be big," make me "feel good," and "take care of things." In exchange, I adored him and solemnly swore that I would never, ever, make him live outside of Manhattan. I think I have that promise in writing somewhere.

Doug regularly fulfilled his three promises (and relished reminding me which one he was accomplishing). He was "big" when he carried the heavy luggage at the airport and "took care of things" when he interrupted a business meeting to call a plumber about an overflowing washing machine because I was too flummoxed by the rising water. For all of this, I did my best to make our home a safe, calm space with minimal demands. I'd left my job as legal counsel at the *New York Times* after Julia was born and worried that my brain would atrophy as a stay-at-home mom. To my surprise, I found that being a wife and mother full-time was the most fulfilling job I'd ever had. Doug made me feel that what I was doing mattered, and nothing made me happier than creating a safe haven in which we could nest. I made sure that, after work, he could move effortlessly from the kids to dinner to a late basketball league game to falling asleep to *Law & Order*. I attended Knicks games at Madison Square Garden (Doug, a rabid fan, shared season tickets with a college buddy) and dutifully *rewatched* them on videotape when we got home, so Doug could share his analysis of important plays with an attentive listener. I learned to respect Doug's sometimes exasperating passion for the Knicks—I will never forget making the mistake of attempting to read the *New York Post* at the Garden during a particularly uneventful game against the Mavericks (a weak team at the time). Doug tore the paper out of my hands and threw it to the ground. "What?" I asked incredulously. "Why do you care? You never talk to me during games." He answered with a semi-serious growl, "In the event I want to discuss a play or point out a mismatch, you *must* know what I'm talking about." After that moment, I always paid rapt attention. Our life worked—again, unbearably cliché, but true. I always described our relationship to people that way. "It's like breathing," I'd say.

At breakfast, Doug took out the video camera: "It's September eleventh, do you know what we're doing today?" The kids giggled and asked Daddy to turn the video screen around so that they could see themselves. He asked them to name their teachers and describe what they looked forward to doing at school. The kids giggled and blew kisses at the camera while I, clad in a frumpy terry cloth bathrobe, scrupulously avoided the lens. Doug swooped over to the stove where I was ladling pancake mix onto a skillet and wrapped his arms around my waist. "I'll see you tonight for Grandpa's dinner. It's going to be great. You're the one." My gentle husband of six and a half years—in his new blue shirt—tousled my hair and kissed me good-bye. Michael walked his daddy to the door to press the elevator button as he did every morning. I heard Doug hug his son in a loud squeeze, then Doug was gone.

Gone.

That simple word can be so benign—when someone leaves a room, he's *gone,* when your toddler eats her carrots, they're *all gone.* Doug went to work and was *gone* in the usual way. Until he wasn't. Until that *gone* became something else entirely, just a few hours later. *Gone* became "vanished," "lost," "evaporated." It was the worst *gone* that I'd ever known, and when I replayed it (how many times have I gone back over that morning?), all I can think of is that, if I had it to do over, I'd have dug my fingers into that blue shirt and never let go.

I got Michael ready for school. Forty-five minutes later, we stood in our building's lobby as I took pictures of my ebullient son grinning in his green, tie-dyed T-shirt and khaki shorts. He grabbed my hand, high-fived the doorman, and we trotted out onto the sunny sidewalk for the short walk around the corner.

When the world fell apart, I was unaware. While downtown burned, I watched Michael work a puzzle in his classroom. I was snapping pictures of him and his teacher when my sitter, Glenda, appeared in the doorway with Julia in her arms. I was later told that Glenda was screaming my name while she was running through the hallways, but I only remember her telling me, "Jen, you need to go home. A plane hit the Trade Center, but Joe [Doug's dad] said Doug was getting out." I had no idea what she was saying. I heard her continue, "Go home and call Doug." I left Glenda with the kids and started to walk down the four flights to the sidewalk. My cell phone wasn't working, but at that point, I wasn't worried. What's the big deal? Some single-engine got misdirected and clipped the tower? I continued to try to reach Doug to no avail as I walked around the corner toward my apartment building. In the lobby, I asked our doorman, Ney, "What's this about a plane and the Trade Center?" Only when the last word came out of my mouth did I notice Ney's face. He was ashen, he couldn't meet my eyes. My stomach turned over. I hurried upstairs, clicked on the television, and watched my life end.

Doug's colleague, a young manager from Cantor whom Doug mentored, suddenly appeared at my door. He'd bicycled over to wait with me. I took that as a bad sign. It instantly reminded me of movie scenes in which the military officer arrives at the white clapboard house to deliver tragic news about a soldier—the wife knows the minute she sees the dark sedan pull into her driveway; her world collapses without a line of dialogue.

The phone started ringing incessantly. I was standing in our dark kitchen with the breakfast dishes still piled in the sink, talking to Doug's friend from college, Michael Kaminer. He called from Boston a few moments before I saw the South Tower collapse. On television, the imploding building roared to earth, and I watched a storm of dust and debris belch out of the wreckage. Michael pleaded on the phone through my screams, "What's going on?"

"He's dead," I announced, and hung up. I couldn't stay on the line another second. Doug was on the 105th floor of the North Tower. It hadn't yet fallen, but I knew he was gone. I felt him leave me, slam out of my chest like an astronaut hurtling into space with a torn lifeline. Several years later, an audio recording of Doug's cell phone call to 911 at about the time of the South Tower collapse surfaced and confirmed the accuracy of my experience. A representative from the mayor's office called to tell me that Doug was one of only a handful of people in the towers identified on the 911 tapes from that day. The city would be sending the tapes to the "next of kin," but she advised that I, specifically, should not listen to Doug's recording by myself. She told me that it was "horrific," and Doug's voice was "excruciating" to hear. With my heart pounding so loud I could hear it, I asked whether she could send a written transcript so I wouldn't have to listen to it at all. She replied officiously that the city wasn't making transcriptions; they were only providing CDs. I couldn't believe my ears. Was this bureaucrat actually telling me that we would have to pop a disc into a laptop to hear our husbands' wretched final utterances? I launched into an onslaught of finely articulated fury at the city's callous lack of judgment: "Do you have any idea the impact this will have on a widow when she receives just a recording without a transcript? How can she not listen to it? You can't just inflict these tapes upon us without giving us a choice about how we experience them." The poor woman stuttered and tried to tell me she understood how I felt. "I don't need your understanding. I need you to tell your supervisors to provide transcripts, or I swear I will call every media outlet in New York and expose the city's asinine refusal to type a few write-ups so we might not have to hear our husbands' tortured voices screaming from the grave!" Three days later, the woman called to let me know that written transcripts would be included with the tapes.

I never listened to Doug's voice. I did read the neatly typed transcript, tentatively, holding the page away from my face at an oblique angle so that my eyes gleaned only a few words at a time. I don't know for sure, but I think he died on the phone while asking how long it would take for help to arrive. At the end, he was still trying to take care of things. I know some people can't fathom why, to this day, I've never chosen to hear my husband's last words. But I knew that I could never survive the sound of his suffering. I'd already imagined Doug's agony and fear a thousand times—I put myself with him, wrapping my body around his in the smoky chaos while the floors collapsed. I eventually locked those replayed scenarios away in a deep corner of my mind. To hear Doug's voice—his soothing, gravelly baritone distorted into a choked, desperate whisper—would literally destroy me. I gave the tape and transcript to my younger sister, Jayme, to hide them somewhere out of reach. I didn't want his last words lying around where I could access them in a weak moment.

·····

I spent another few seconds watching the South Tower cave and stumbled my way out of the kitchen into the family room. Sunlight streamed in the side window through the partially closed blinds, the view obstructed by construction scaffolding that felt as if it'd been up forever, as workers repaired the aging façade. I stood there, looking at the happy photographs and children's books crowding the shelves of the built-in bookcase, at the L-shaped sofa with "Doug's corner," where he always stretched out. I remember how bleak the house felt at that moment. With one hand on the couch, I lowered myself to my knees and heard myself say, "Doug's gone. I'm a widow." I repeated it, maniacally, like a madwoman, as I dialed Doug's sister, Danielle, who lived downtown. "My life is over," I said simply. "Come up here when you can."

My friend Pamela Weinberg arrived next. She came directly from Stephen Wise where her son, Benjamin, attended with Michael. Pam is one of my closest friends. I met her about five years earlier at a local manicure place on Amsterdam Avenue. We were both pregnant with our sons at the time, and she had just coauthored the first in a series of successful *City Baby* books and hosted weekly new-mother seminars around Manhattan. Sitting at the nail dryers, we bonded over weight gain, weak bladders, and swollen feet. Our boys were born five weeks apart in the fall of 1996. Pam was the ultimate girly girl. Petite, with long, wavy, light brown hair and the warmest smile, she was the best friend who organized spa days with the girls, cried during romantic comedies no matter how corny, and hosted mother/daughter reading groups in her traditionally appointed home. She brought a Martha Stewart quality to everything she did, minus the New England hauteur. Thank God for Pam. Without her I would never have discovered the frozen yogurt at Bloomingdale's or learned how to make the perfect spinach dip.

Pam ran to me in the family room, and I felt her arms around me. Her eyes looked wild as they searched my face for news. I told her Doug was dead. She tried calmly to convince me that he might be walking up the West Side Highway with the other survivors. I shook my head and pounded my chest, "He's dead, Pam. I can't feel him anymore."

My parents called from their home in Longmeadow. They could barely speak. My dad's voice sounded so small to me. My mother told me that they were trying to figure out the fastest way to get to Manhattan. They'd heard that the city had closed all bridges, tunnels, and roads. I told them to come tomorrow—there was nothing they could do now.

Jayme, my only sibling, called from St. Vincent's hospital on Twelfth Street, where she worked as a pediatric nurse practitioner. Her practice concentrated primarily on treating children and adolescents with HIV/AIDS. As I often said, my sister was a saint, saving the world while I was out to conquer it. Jayme and I were as close as two sisters could be, and she loved Doug as a brother. The two of them were at my side while I gave birth to

Michael and Julia, with Jayme cajoling Doug through the process and giving him a strong shoulder on which to lean when his nerves began to fray. From the day our son was born, Doug addressed my sister only as "Aunt Jayme" and counted on her to walk him through every sniffle, cough, bump, and bruise.

Jayme was being held at the hospital to wait for injured victims, but almost no one materialized. No victims. No injuries. Either you got out unscathed or you perished. In or out. Gone or still here. No in-between. She arrived at my apartment in the late afternoon. I hung up the phone and ran back to Stephen Wise, where I'd left the kids. My upstairs neighbor, Margie, was walking through the synagogue's lobby with her children. I grabbed her by the shoulders and literally barked at her to find Michael and Julia and take them to her apartment. She recoiled, confused by my brusqueness, and told me to calm down, "Easy, we're all a bit tense right now." I snapped through clenched teeth, "Margie, it's Doug!" She'd forgotten my husband worked in the Trade Center. She suddenly looked just like my doorman: stunned, pale, speechless. For months, I would see the same reaction on every face in front of me.

For the next several hours, my home morphed into a command center. In addition to my friends and Doug's family, who crowded into the apartment to wait with me for news, families and friends of Cantor employees called all day, expecting I'd have answers because Doug was a senior partner. But he wasn't in charge anymore, and I had no special intelligence just because he'd been the boss. Doug was just as dead as everyone else.

I never understood pacing until I couldn't stop; all I could manage was to walk from the family room to my bedroom and back. Doug's father and mother fell into the same tread, shuffling between the living room and family room. Doug's sister scanned the Internet. Pam made phone calls from the kitchen. No one ate or drank. No one spoke except to offer a theory about how Doug might still be alive. That was one thing I could not handle. Any reference to Doug as "missing" undid me. He was dead. It didn't help to hypothesize some miraculous escape. I didn't want to read the hundreds of e-mails with useless updates. "I heard the 86th floor got out." Doug was on the 105th. "He could be badly burned and unidentified in a hospital in New Jersey." Impossible. Too many e-mails opened with "Please tell me Doug got out." I replied to every note or comment the same way: "He's gone." All I could focus on was one looming task: how was I going to tell Michael and Julia that Daddy was never coming home?

Each time the phone rang, heads whipped around and everyone stared at me, hoping that Doug was somehow on the line. I answered every call, trying not to allow myself to believe that he was safe. I spoke with several newly minted widows that morning—together, we'd joined a wretched club of which we wanted no part. LaChanze Gooding, the accomplished Broadway actress and wife of Doug's college pal Calvin, called several times. Her husband worked on the 103rd floor running Cantor's Emerging Markets division. She and Calvin had been married less than three years, and she was eight months pregnant with their second daughter. I unabashedly adored Calvin. And Calvin loved his friends with unrestrained emotion. He and Doug played basketball together at Haverford and served as ushers at each other's wedding. His wedding to LaChanze was the most joyous, emotionally effusive event I'd ever attended, complete with African dancers, Ghanaian marriage rituals and impromptu jam sessions by LaChanze's musically gifted friends. When Calvin and I last spoke, he told me he was writing a hilarious tribute song to perform at Doug's fortieth birthday dinner celebration. Now, with a deep pit in my stomach, I tried to reassure LaChanze unconvincingly that we would get each other through this. She was certain Calvin was missing, that he might have gotten out of the building. I feared he was as gone as my husband, but I didn't say anything. I just said that I loved her and whatever happened, Doug and Calvin were together.

The house didn't stop. Tense conversations in low tones incessantly buzzed. I heard my sister-in-law say that she couldn't handle looking at the photos of Doug on the walls. Neither could I. There he was, smiling at the camera, cradling a tiny Julia in his large arms or tossing a squealing Michael into the air at the beach. How often have we seen similar photos on newscasts? Murder victims who became smiling snapshots on CNN. Was Doug now just a human-interest story? One of the chilling total killed on a late-summer morning? I retreated to my bedroom in the early afternoon, unable to find a quiet corner anywhere else. Pam stood sentinel at the doorway, allowing visitors to pass at her discretion. I remember sobbing on the shoulder of my cousin when Allison burst through the door.

Allison was married to Doug's best friend, Howard Lutnick, president and chairman of Cantor Fitzgerald. He survived the attacks that morning because he had taken his oldest son, Kyle, to his first day of kindergarten. The Lutnick and Gardner families were entwined—their children and ours overlapped in ages, and we shared nearly all of our family vacations and holidays together.

I was especially close with Allison, whom I first met on Doug's thirty-second birthday in 1993, at a Cantor Fitzgerald party at the Metropolitan Museum of Art. The party was one in a series of events celebrating the opening of the Iris and B. Gerald Cantor Roof Garden, a gift from the founder of Cantor Fitzgerald, Bernie Cantor. Doug and I had been dating for about six weeks. I arrived straight from work, and as soon as we ascended the grand steps on Fifth Avenue leading into the museum, I could tell this was going to be one of those corporate bacchanals that were legendary in New York at that time. The party spilled through the Egyptian gallery into the magnificent Temple of Dendur. Inside, guests shoveled caviar onto toast points from overflowing stations and enjoyed trays of shrimp, Peking duck, and other delicacies I couldn't afford. The room twinkled with hundreds of candles. Cascading flowers and crystal-laden tables were everywhere. Cantor even hired a limousine service to carry guests home in black town cars after the party. I stood sipping champagne, wearing a well-worn, green Kenar suit picked up at a sample sale, and Nine West black patent leather pumps. Not exactly Cinderella, but I did feel a bit like Dorothy.

We didn't have caviar, museum openings, or surgically enhanced dowagers flaunting tablespoon-size diamonds in the unassuming neighborhoods of Massachusetts where I was raised. We'd lived a typical, middle-class existence of car pools, basement birthday parties, and family dinners at Friendly's. My mother taught in the public schools and my father worked in advertising. Our family vacations typically entailed camping, skiing local mountains, or fishing on Cape Cod. Once we took a ten-day trip to Florida, four of which were spent driving from Massachusetts to Orlando and back in a Pontiac Grand Safari station wagon (with the requisite wood paneling on the sides.) I financed my entire law school education at Harvard through two different student loans.

Fashion and style were not part of my vocabulary. Instead of *Vogue* and *Harper's Bazaar,* I grew up reading *Sports Illustrated, Time,* and *Mad* magazine. My underdeveloped sartorial tastes ranged from the Limited to Filene's Basement. An Ann Taylor suit eventually became the holy grail of my wardrobe, as

I stretched my budget to invest in a few proper outfits for law firm interviews and my fledgling career. Still, I didn't have a clue about style. It got so bad that a paralegal at work, a woman who made half my salary but dressed with a practiced eye, took me to lunch one day for the sole purpose of forcing me to buy two pairs of decent shoes. Then she unceremoniously tossed my cracked, boring pumps in the nearest trash can.

When Howard saw us enter the Temple of Dendur that night, he came straight over with outstretched arms and a big smile. He'd just played golf with Doug and two Knicks basketball players that morning, a gift Howard generously bid on at a charity auction for Doug's birthday.

Howard Lutnick exudes confidence and brio. He was forced to grow up quickly when his father died of complications from chemotherapy during the first week of Howard's freshman year at Haverford. Howard's mother had died the previous year from cancer. At eighteen years old, he and his older sister, Edie (a law student at the time), were orphaned and suddenly responsible for their fourteen-year-old brother, Gary. Who could have predicted that Howard's early tragedies would serve as a warm-up for the catastrophic events to come?

Eventually, all three siblings finished school and moved to New York for their careers. Howard joined Cantor Fitzgerald as a bond trader and soon became Bernie Cantor's protégé. Bernie named Howard president of the firm when he was only twenty-nine years old, and Howard has helmed the firm for over twenty years. Howard saw Cantor as an extension of his family and hired his brother to work with him. He recruited his friends (and their friends and family members) because, as he liked to say, "if we're going to spend so much time working so hard, we might as well do it with people we love." This made Cantor an attractive environment, but also compounded the tragedy that would come. At least twenty sets of "doubles"—parent/child or sibling pairs—died that day in the North Tower, along with golf foursomes, fishing buddies, and fraternity brothers.

After hugging Doug and clapping him on the shoulder, Howard shook my hand and greeted me with an edgy smile that said, "I'm glad you make my friend happy, but I need to know more." Howard launched into an interrogation that fell somewhere between playful cocktail chatter and a Star Chamber. I bobbed and parried and hoped I held my own.

Howard walked us over to where his then girlfriend, Allison, was sitting with her parents. Allison stood up, and I felt sure she was the most glamorous woman I'd ever seen. A thick, shiny mane of jet-black hair spilled over her delicate shoulders framing bright eyes, sculpted cheekbones, and glossed lips. She stood before me, lithe and impeccable in designer clothes I couldn't identify. I felt instantly drab in my green suit as Allison smiled warmly and reached out her elegant hand. Why was I surprised that Howard was dating the Jewish version of a supermodel? To make matters worse, she was sincere, intelligent, and not a lady who lunched: Allison was an accomplished litigator who would soon become a partner at a large insurance defense firm. I tucked my hand under Doug's arm and tried to stand up straight.

When Doug joined Cantor a few months after the Met party, Allison's and my lives merged. Howard and Allison got engaged three months before we did. Our weddings were four months apart (they were married at the Plaza, we at the Essex House). We spoke every day and quickly got to where we understood each other without having to complete a sentence. It turned out she and I came from similar backgrounds and struggled with tight budgets like every other new arrival during our first few years in the city. We were both crossing the threshold from girlfriend to wife together and delighted to have a trusted side-kick. Looking back, we had a kind of halcyon routine: The men worked together contentedly, and we coordinated our lives to keep our families together. We attended every Cantor social function together and took joint vacations to Florida, the Caribbean, and Europe. Our first sons were born six months apart and then our second children within a year of each other. Allison and I compiled impressive pregnancy wardrobes, which we stored in plastic boxes by season and shuttled the growing collection back and forth. We found in each other a "secret sharer" when it came to food. Unlike my weight-conscious friends who refused to eat more than a dry salad in public, Allison and I never met a bread basket we didn't devour. An e-mail of "I'm hungry, where are you?" would prompt an immediate rendezvous at the local diner for tuna melts, or, if we had the time, a favorite Italian place for a more leisurely lunch of rigatoni *butera* and *caprese* salad with thick slabs of mozzarella. I happily endured extra hours on the treadmill to pay for these indulgences, but Allison, the genetic miracle, maintained her waiflike figure with nary a sit-up.

Being a Cantor wife was a little like being in *The Sopranos.* We learned quickly to accept without complaint our husbands' long hours at work, their overseas business trips and road shows, the curtailed vacations, and the frequent Sunday meetings. Our men were busy, working hard to build their business and share with their families the fruits of their success. Allison and I had an insider's view of life as a Cantor wife; we were a two-person support group, a loyal partnership through which we could divulge and vent freely in confidence.

Among the four of us, there was no such thing as too much

information—the personal details of our marriages that we shared to raucous laughter over late-night drinks might make some shake their heads, but for us, this intimate familiarity was the secret language of our merry foursome. The term *happy marriage* seems flat or too simple, but it's apt; it's what we each had. The Lutnicks and Gardners were happy. Until we were despondent.

When Allison flew into my bedroom that early afternoon of September 11, I knew that I had lost more than Doug. The Gardner/Lutnick balance, our idyllic history, was finished. We were no longer equals; my life had fallen off a cliff while she and her intact family continued to move forward. This altered dynamic rocked our friendship during the next few months, creating for me an unprecedented discomfort and confusion that took time to reconcile.

Allison wrapped herself around me, and we both sobbed into each other's shoulders, twisting in pain. The only other time I saw her like that was three years prior in the emergency room after Kyle accidentally cracked his head open on their marble floor. We resolved that unfortunate mishap with a few dozen stitches. How would we ever fix this? I noticed that she was wearing running shoes and not her signature heels. Her sneakers were perfectly white and had probably never met the sidewalk, since Allison was not known to jog. "What are those?" I asked, pointing to her unexpected footwear. She looked down. "I ran through Central Park to get here."

"You *ran?*"

"The streets are closed. I had to get to you."

"Where's Howard? Your sitter told me he was going to the Trade Center."

"He's down there. He went straight from Kyle's school."

"It's bad, isn't it?"

The tears spilled over Allison's distressed face. "It's as bad as it can possibly be."

"I know." I started to choke again. "What are we going to do?" No answers, just tears.

Allison left after a while to return to her frightened children. About an hour after she'd gone, Howard walked through the front door, shattered. He was covered in cement dust, dirt, and other matter I didn't want to investigate. We held on to each other in the foyer for a long time; he repeated in my ear forcefully, "You'll be fine. I promise, you will be fine!" Neither of us tried to paint an optimistic picture. He'd just had a front-row seat to the North Tower's collapse. The firm was wiped out in seconds, and Howard's brother, Gary, who was with Doug at the office that morning, was among the dead. I told my friend I knew we wouldn't be seeing each other much in the next few weeks; he had a colossal task ahead of him. Howard nodded, "I have to take care of my families." Cantor lost 658 employees, the greatest toll suffered by any single company that day. Clearly, Howard wasn't going to have time to mourn his brother and best friend—there was so much loss in front of him and so many decisions.

In the next few weeks, I would see Howard only sporadically, but he called whenever he could grab a few minutes. We talked in the middle of the night or while he was traveling from one deceased employee's home to another. In some ways, I was Howard's canary in the coal mine; whatever I was feeling at any given time—fear, insecurity, fury—gave him a vivid picture of how the families were coping. Allison, too, was pulled into the vortex of grieving families and a chaotic household that had transformed into Cantor's makeshift headquarters. Distraught family members and the press bombarded their phone lines, faxes, and e-mail accounts seeking information about the victims or what Cantor was doing to help. Within a day of the attacks, Allison presciently set up the company's crisis center at a local hotel, where the families could gather to see Howard and receive whatever bits of information Cantor had. She also recruited friends and volunteers to answer phones, do errands, and organize information at her home, while Howard and his remaining partners struggled to run the firm from the dining room.

Allison called every day, but I knew she was overwhelmed with trying to take care of her husband and the families of so many people she loved and admired. More than anything I wished I could have been more helpful to her, to shoulder half the burden, offer comfort and empathy. But Doug was dead, and I couldn't see beyond my own suffering. I was helpless and useless. I tried to spend an evening at the crisis center, but the crowds and panicked faces sent me reeling. Allison hurried me out of the ballroom with one arm protectively wrapped around my shoulder and made sure someone took me home. It killed me that I was too weak to be there for her. All I could do was admire her strength under such intense pressure and pray that we would one day find our way back.

After Howard left my apartment, I remembered to call Shun Lee and cancel our dinner reservation and a doctor's appointment scheduled for Thursday. I actually told the doctor's receptionist in a strangely calm voice that I couldn't make it because my husband had just died in the Trade Center. I wondered if she received other similar calls that week. I then asked Jayme to call my neighbor. "Please ask Margie to send the kids home now." Jayme nodded, the tears forming in her eyes, and I stumbled to the bedroom. I arranged some pillows against the headboard and seated myself on our bed. *Our bed*. Now it was just mine.

Only a week ago Doug had gathered all of us together right under this comforter upon hearing the news that a local restaurant owner had died in a car accident. Doug declared, "That's it, no one is ever leaving this bed. We're going to stay right here forever." Our bed. Home base. We're safe. Not anymore. For the next several months I'd sleep, if at all, with my face pressed against my nightstand, turned away from Doug's side.

Jayme led Michael and Julia into the bedroom. Michael was still wearing his clothes from school. Julia had a big white bow in her hair. Just two mornings ago I found Doug in Julia's bedroom, sitting on the carpet as he tried to affix one of Julia's ubiquitous bows to her downy hair. Julia wasn't cooperating, squirming in his arms and dashing away in sheer delight that Daddy couldn't catch her. I noticed she had also thrown several dresses and T-shirts out of their drawers onto the floor. Doug looked at me helplessly amid the detritus of our toddler's reverie. With an exaggerated frown on his face, he whimpered, "Honey, our daughter refuses to get dressed."

"Douglas," I said, trying not to laugh at the precious scene. "You're the adult. Who's in charge here?"

He looked admiringly at his cackling daughter and pointed. "She is. I'm just a toy."

Could it have been two days ago? Now, these two wide-eyed, giggly babies climbed over me and settled under my arms. I didn't want to see their bright little faces go dark. I hugged and kissed them for a while, holding them close and inhaling their sweetness as if I were taking in my last breaths before drowning. Michael said, "Grandma is in the living room." I looked down at his curious brown eyes and said, "I have to tell you something important." I fought the lump growing in my throat. "There was a big explosion at Daddy's office building. It was very bad, and we can't find Daddy." Julia played with my hair. Michael's brown eyes grew wide. He asked me if Daddy got out. "I don't think so, Michael. Daddy is very strong and he tried really hard, but I think it was just so bad and sudden and he didn't have time." Michael looked up at me and said, "I'm going to sit with Grandma."

My in-laws left the apartment when it was dark. I did that pacing thing again through the house with my sister for several hours. Glenda, our sitter, fed the kids dinner and turned on *Blue's Clues*. I tried to bathe Michael and Julia at bedtime, but Jayme had to finish the task. I didn't have the strength or the smiles, and I didn't want them to feel the weight. My mind raced, making it impossible to sit still. My skin felt tight and ill-fitting, like a scratchy wool dress on a hot day. I looked out our second-story window at a dark and eerily deserted Central Park West. Only a few cars passed. On many warm nights Doug would call from the back of a taxi on his way home from work and ask me to bring the kids to the front window. I would hold Michael and Julia in their pajamas up to the glass and say, "Let's look for Daddy!" We would count yellow cabs until one would stop across the street, and Doug would emerge with his heavy briefcase under the street lamp. The kids would shout for Daddy through the plate glass, and Doug would look up in mock surprise, blow kisses, and dash inside. Now, our treasured routine was just a memory, one in a sea of moments big and small that we would never be able to share again.

I don't even remember if I put the kids to bed that night—I think Jayme did it because I was shaking too much. My sister helped me get ready for bed. I didn't want to get undressed. If I took off my clothes, the day would be over, the possibility of a different ending extinguished. Doug always came home at the end of the day. What happened to him?

I couldn't breathe. I ranted to Jayme that I wished it were

a year from now. "A year from now it has to be better, right? I can't do this. I can't feel like this for another minute. Please, just make it a year from now." I wanted to get out of my skin, to shed the day's horror and escape back to yesterday. I wanted Doug to come home, to hear the front door open and the sound of change clattering onto the foyer table. I sent Doug an e-mail—"I love you. You did everything right."

Jayme slept next to me. I don't think I slept much, but when I did, terrifying images of burning buildings and stampeding crowds hurled through my brain. My body continued to tremble and the painful hole in my stomach expanded. I spent the predawn hours sitting next to Michael's bed on his blue carpet staring at the painted baseball knobs on his white bureau. When I heard him stir around 6:00 a.m., I sat down on his comforter with the dancing teddy bears and waited for him to open his eyes. I knew it was coming. "Did Daddy come home?" I told him no. He sat up and said, "Mommy, maybe he couldn't come home because the streetlight broke. Maybe the light won't change to green, and Daddy can't cross the street." I got Michael dressed and took him with his bicycle across the street to the parking lot of Tavern on the Green. Doug had recently taught him to ride a two-wheeler—an accomplishment about which Doug proudly boasted to anyone within earshot. Michael rode around me in a silent circle for a while and then stopped. "Maybe the plane flew too low because a stewardess tripped when she served the food, and the pilot tried to help." I explained to him that bad people were flying the plane, and that this was not an accident. "Was Daddy running when he tried to get out? Did he try to jump out of the way?" I told him that the explosion was too powerful, and Daddy's office was too high. Michael looked up at me and said, "I think Daddy died."

Michael and I visited Tavern on the Green's parking lot for

the next three mornings. He would ride, I would answer. Sometimes he would tell me, "I'm strong, Mommy. I could have gotten out." He wanted to know why Daddy didn't jump, or why no ladder was outside his window. He reassured himself, "Airplanes can't hit our building because we live on the second floor, right?" He sounded as if he could have been asking why birds fly or why the sky is blue. Except, in this case, I didn't have any intelligent answers. Mommy and Me classes don't teach you how to explain to a five-year-old that Daddy was murdered in his office by terrorists. I knew instinctively, however, that my son needed the facts without adornment. He needed to know that Daddy would never leave us on purpose, he was taken away unfairly. I just explained, "Daddy didn't have time, he tried really hard to come home to us, and we're proud of him."

·····

The days and weeks following Doug's death moved at an unbearably slow pace. It wasn't easy for me to make sense of my new status. I am Jennifer Gardner, Doug Gardner's wife. I *was* Doug Gardner's wife. I'm still his wife, but he's dead. I'm single, but I'm married. I'm married, but I have no husband. Doug was my husband, but he's gone. I'm a widow. What is that? Widow . . . widow . . . widow . . . that word pervaded my thoughts like an insidious virus. Widow-maker, widow's walk, widow's peak, black widow, *The Merry Widow*. The dictionary defines *widow* as "to separate, to divide." That's true. I was, unquestionably, irrevocably separated and divided from the beautiful life we'd had before. From now on, my life would be demarcated with a Before and After; every memory tagged with one of those distinct labels. Could I really be a widow so soon? For me, widow was just the last box on a medical form at the doctor's office: Single, Married, Separated, Divorced, Widowed. Widowed is always listed last because who the hell is widowed? I never really noticed that word, but now it was as if it were flashing in neon wherever I turned.

Who is a widow? An ancient Italian woman from the *Godfather* movies dressed in black under a veil? World War II wives in shirtwaist dresses receiving horrible news via telegram? The kaffeeklatsch of Jewish ladies in Boca playing canasta? How can this term possibly apply to me? I was a thirty-five-year-old lawyer raising two small children on the Upper West Side. I'm happily married, for God's sake. I was definitely not going to get through this.

At least I wasn't alone in Widowville. Turning on the television, I could see that, post-9/11, widows weren't such a rare commodity anymore. No longer were we hidden away, only venturing out in the company of girlfriends. We weren't required to raise our children dutifully while maintaining a quiet distance from the world. Instead, widows were on every talk show and news update, petitioning Congress and City Hall to preserve, redesign, or sanctify Ground Zero. Apparently, we were a hot trend, the new black. We had cachet—at least as far as the media and politicians were concerned. Paraded around State of the Union addresses, honored at charity functions, and remembered at Super Bowl games, the 9/11 widows became every politician's or social climber's favorite accessory.

I didn't have the strength to join the fight for better security measures or a proper memorial at Ground Zero. Thankfully, other brave families did. I knew myself. I'd have pursued the cause single-mindedly and would never have been able to extricate my soul from a bottomless pit of fury and despair. I feared I'd lose myself in the process and diminish Doug if I focused on how he died instead of remembering how he lived. I could neither live at his grave nor attempt to achieve mythical "closure" and move on; how I lived without Doug would never be a black-or-white proposition. I needed not to choose and simply try to muddle through the gray.

Although I avoided most of the media frenzy, I did receive my share of sideshow curiosity from the sympathetic but ever-inquisitive young mothers swirling about the Upper East and West Sides of Manhattan. I've been pointed out at my children's school and whispered about at the gym or on the street: "That's her over there. That one, she lost her husband on 9/11. I like her shoes." No one meant any malice by it, of course. I was just a marked woman, the girl sporting the Scarlet W on her chest. I was visible, useful social currency to be exchanged over manicures or lunch at Saks. I was the embodiment of everyone else's fears. There but for the grace of God go I.

The media feasted on every detail of the catastrophe. Protecting the kids from the violent images became my full-time job. The news constantly replayed the moments the planes struck the buildings. We perused daily the *New York Times* section, "A Nation Challenged," for those who perished so that Michael and Julia could see they were not the only ones to lose a daddy. Every morning we read the short biographical stories under each victim's picture. Michael memorized the names of all the companies that lost employees. We identified Daddy's close friends who died with him—Calvin Gooding, Gary Lutnick, Greg Richards, Joe Shea, Andy Kates, Fred Varacchi, Jeff Goldflam, Dave Bauer, Eric Sand, Doug Gurian. Sadly, there were hundreds more friends and colleagues to count. After a few weeks of our morning routine, every time Julia saw a headshot in the newspaper, she asked if the person had died.

Michael began to own the story of his father's death. He told his friends what happened, repeating the words that I had spoken to him. At school, Benjamin Weinberg, Pam's son, attached himself to Michael. Wherever Michael turned, Benjamin, like a tiny Secret Service agent, was at his side. He made sure that the other children didn't raise the subject unless Michael wanted to talk about it. Once, when the students were painting on a table covered with used newspapers, Michael saw a photograph of a billboard that displayed the names of some of the victims. Shockingly, he saw his father's name on the billboard and pointed it out to his classmates. Some of the children tried to argue with Michael, insisting that his dad didn't die. Benjamin shielded him and stopped the other kids' challenges. To this day, Benjamin and Michael are inseparable.

·····

On the one-year anniversary of Doug's death, Michael attended his first day of kindergarten at Riverdale Country School, a private school in the Bronx just north of Manhattan. Doug had graduated from Riverdale in 1979 and decreed to me that his children would continue the Gardner legacy at his alma mater. Although he good-naturedly permitted me to explore other schools in the city, he'd already decided his children would be Riverdalians. Indeed, on our spring tour, Doug delighted in pointing out his former hangouts and the locations where he suffered his various injuries, including a low ceiling on which he banged his head, and the nurse's office where Nurse Boyle once diagnosed him with appendicitis. As with most things, Doug was right about Riverdale. It was a beautiful school nestled on several acres of green fields and mature trees. The school reminded me of a small college campus, but with playground equipment and children's artwork taped in each window. Doug couldn't wait for his children to sit in the same classrooms and walk the same halls he did as a student. We mailed Michael's application to Riverdale the weekend before the attacks.

New York private schools conduct interviews with applicants and their families in the fall before making enrollment decisions. I knew I couldn't handle those interviews, waiting alone, the weepy widow, alongside well-coiffed couples holding hands and watching overdressed four-year-olds smile stiffly for the admissions officers. I also started fretting about sending Michael to school in the Bronx; Riverdale was too far outside Manhattan and I worried about reaching him if there was another attack. Just a few weeks after 9/11, Pam arranged an interview for Michael at Dalton, her daughter's school on the Upper East Side, which was a mere cab ride from my apartment. She told my story to Dalton's head of admissions, Elizabeth Krents, and explained that I was having second thoughts about sending Michael to his father's school. Ms. Krents graciously allowed me to sob on her couch for a half hour while Michael met with the admissions staff. She told me to stay in touch in case I decided against Riverdale.

When it came time for Michael to have his interview at Riverdale, Doug had been gone for just two months. Walking alone with my child up the leafy path from the parking lot to the admissions building took every ounce of strength I had. The receptionist ushered Michael into an office where Dan DiVirgilio, the admissions director, welcomed him with a big smile. Everyone knew our story, but thankfully no one said a word while I waited on the couch outside the office. After ten minutes, Mr. DiVirgilio called me in. A rumpled older man with intelligent eyes and a benevolent smile, he offered me a seat on the leather chair across from his desk. While Michael played with an abacus in the corner, he asked me how I was coping. Big mistake. The façade cracked and choked sobs burst out, causing the poor man to dive for the Kleenex box and wait uncomfortably while I regained a modicum of composure. He told me what a beautiful and intelligent boy Michael was and assured me that he was a good fit with Riverdale. I was distraught. How could I sit there talking about our son's education at Doug's school without Doug? The interview process was too much for me; I begged Mr. DiVirgilio to make a decision soon so that I could be done with this agonizing and lonely ordeal.

Two weeks later, I received a call from Riverdale that Mr. DiVirgilio had died suddenly of a heart attack. *Of course he did.* In the absurd world in which I now lived, why wouldn't my son's interviewer drop dead right before admissions decisions were made? I half-expected boils and dead livestock next. What's worse, my first panicked thought was not "How sad" but "Please, God, tell me he took notes." I suppressed my alarm long enough to offer hurried condolences to the voice on the other end of the phone—silently begging Michael to forgive me for being a heartless mother—and then asked, "I know this may seem rather self-centered at a time like this, but do Michael and I have to go through this process again? Did he take enough notes for you to make a decision?" I never told Michael what happened, but Riverdale accepted him soon after, and Doug's son joined the class of 2015.

It was nearly unbearable to walk Michael across campus without Doug, a year after the attacks, that precarious first day. Another missed first day of school in a long line of missed milestones to come. They didn't get easier as time passed—Michael's first basketball game, Julia's school plays, birthdays, Thanksgivings, fifth-grade graduation, a bar mitzvah—each moment a joyous occasion, but etched with the pale reminders of an absent father. As we walked to Michael's classroom together, I worried about how strangers would treat him, how Michael would handle being the only child at the school at the time who had lost a parent in the World Trade Center. Moms and dads sat together with their cameras in the back of the classroom as Ms. Mahony, the kindergarten teacher, greeted her new students. I sat with my mother, and we both held our breath.

A moment of silence marked the moment when the North Tower was struck for the first time. Not surprisingly, the school psychologist positioned himself in our classroom. I fought to restrain my tears so that I could watch my son's reaction to the first public acknowledgment of his father's death. All eyes were on Michael. Suddenly, my little boy sat up straight and declared in a clear voice, "My daddy died on 9/11. Two planes hit the building. He tried to get out, but he didn't have time. My daddy is one of the heroes, and we're proud of him." As the teacher picked herself off the floor and the moms dabbed at their running mascara, my child happily plopped himself down in the block area to build a tower with his new classmates.

2

_____

What do you do the day after your husband dies? I bought a vacuum cleaner. My parents had arrived in the late morning with hastily packed suitcases. My mother said she had to clean the house for shivah, but I needed a new vacuum. At least I had something to do.

We held Doug's memorial service on Sunday, five days after the attacks. I needed to have Doug's service as soon as possible. During those five days my home was overrun with family, friends, and heaping platters of cold bagels and folded deli meats. The television news blared through the apartment, constantly replaying the ghastly images of those buildings collapsing. Each rerun was another cruel false reprieve: "Doug is in there—he might still get out"; and then, of course, the same ending, the same collapse, a relived cataclysm, like my own personal Zapruder film replayed again and again. I heard about New Yorkers frantically contacting news channels, begging them to stop showing the hideous images. I hated hearing the newscasters continue to describe victims as "missing." I understood that many families had not yet come to terms with their losses, but I couldn't endure listening to another person cling to the delusion that her boyfriend was somehow lost in New Jersey.

I avoided the television. The news came to me through phone calls from Sarah, a friend of Doug's who worked in the mayor's office. She was my lifeline during these first few days. She explained to me how the city would handle the immediate aftermath of the attacks. She described rerouted traffic plans, security checkpoints, and the grim procedures for processing the deaths of the victims. The city installed a family information center at Pier 94 on the Hudson River, a macabre convention hall where, instead of jewelry vendors or art galleries displaying their wares, the "vendors" were the Red Cross, health and welfare services, and the coroner's office.

Most important, Sarah helped me accomplish one of the most heart-wrenching administrative tasks I needed to complete—providing samples of Doug's DNA to the police. Instead of requiring me to carry hair samples and old Kleenex to the pier, Sarah personally accompanied a policeman to my apartment to collect what the medical examiner's office needed. My sister led the officer to the playroom, out of my sight, where she swabbed Michael and Julia's mouths for the DNA kits. She then directed the officer to our bathroom, where he placed Doug's comb and toothbrush in a Ziploc bag. My enormous bearlike husband was now reduced to cells on a toothbrush. Was he really just ashes at the bottom of a pile?

Eventually, I did go to the pier at Sarah's instruction to register as next of kin and obtain an identification number. The city used the numbers to catalog recovered personal items and bone fragments. I stood in a long line clutching Doug's passport and our marriage certificate. This could have been a scene ripped from

Monty Python and the Holy Grail—"Bring out yer dead. Bring out yer dead."

My apartment alternated between a house of mourning and a crime scene; I needed to put a period on this madness. Without a body to bury, Doug's loss felt ambiguous. I had to get all of these people out of my house. I appreciated (and needed) the loving support, but I couldn't enter or leave a room without someone asking me if I needed anything. What I needed was our life back, but if I couldn't have that, I wanted my children to have some normalcy, whatever that meant.

According to Jewish law, interment occurs as close to the day of death as possible, but since we weren't burying Doug, it was up to the family to decide when to hold a service. Since I knew that the next several months would require a relentless (but necessary) march of wakes, funerals, memorial services, and shivah calls, I frankly wanted Doug to go first. He deserved a packed room filled with friends and colleagues who were still raw, who hadn't yet been numbed by the sheer number of eulogies on the calendar. We'd lost so many friends on that day, including two members of our wedding party, Howard's brother, and nearly the entire executive roster of Cantor. I knew we were headed for a marathon of sadness, sobbing, and tributes in crowded pews. It may have been selfish, but I didn't want Doug to be just one of the many; his service had to be a singular event and fully attended.

We chose Sunday, September 16, five days after the attacks. It was another wretchedly beautiful fall day, the city bathed in sunshine. Dressed in an austere navy pants suit, I left the apartment with my parents, Jayme, and her fiancé, Scott Feldman, to make the short walk to Stephen Wise Synagogue, the same synagogue where Michael and Julia attended school—the place where Doug and I had recently attended their orientation and where I'd first heard the towers had been hit. "One-stop shopping," I said to myself.

We decided to leave the children at home with Glenda. They were too young to sit through an emotional ceremony, and I worried that the throngs and tears would be too much for them; I had enough anxiety about facing the multitudes myself. But, at the same time, it occurred to me that Michael and Julia might one day fault me for deciding not to bring them. Then, a whole new sadness set in, as I thought ahead to how we'd discuss it someday when they were old enough to talk about it and old enough to have only vague memories of their father. Like a sinister game of Whac-A-Mole, I'd think I knocked out a potential source of pain only to see two or three others immediately pop out of nowhere. No matter how hard I tried or how clever I thought I was, I started to learn I'd never be able to contain the hurt.

As we turned the corner on Sixty-Seventh Street, even I wasn't prepared for what greeted us. Literally *hundreds* of people were assembling outside the synagogue on the street and sidewalks. I recognized many faces in the darkly dressed crowd and tightened my grip on Scott's arm.

At the door, I was relieved to see Pamela and our third Musketeer, Vicky Gottlieb, waiting for us. The two of them had rarely left my side that week and organized the memorial service, allowing me simply to arrive and sit. Vicky, a raven-haired, dyed-in-the-wool New Yorker, was a formidable ally. Usually wearing a finely tailored wardrobe fabulously accessorized with enormous chandelier earrings, a colorful scarf, or striking designer shoes, Vicky was well-known for her loyalty, wise counsel, and sharply honed wit. We met at Lamaze class with our husbands prior to the birth of our oldest children. The instructor asked for a show of hands to identify who among us would attempt to give birth naturally, without an epidural. Everyone's hand shot up, except Vicky's and mine. We looked at each other incredulously—she leaned over and whispered between clenched teeth, "Who the *fuck* are these people?" I loved her immediately. We became instant friends, as did our poor husbands, who had to sit patiently with us watching graphic birthing videos, fighting boredom, and trying desperately to prevent their insufferable wives from alienating the rest of the class.

"Don't get mad at me," Vicky said nervously and gave me a quick kiss, as scores of people made their way through the door. "We bought only one guest book, stupidly thinking it would be enough. We didn't realize how big the crowd would be. People are signing legal pads now because we ran out of room." She sheepishly held up several wrinkled yellow pages of blue signatures. "Unforgivable," I whispered with a small laugh. "And, by the way, I like your lipstick."

Vicky and Pam had come over to help me get dressed the morning after the attacks. While rifling through my makeup drawer Vicky slipped my new Chanel lipstick into her bag. Pam and I, a bit amazed by what we were seeing, asked what she was doing. "What? It's a good pink," she said matter-of-factly. "Besides, Jen, you're not going to be wearing it anytime soon." The three of us still crack up laughing at that purely Vicky moment. Who else but your best girlfriend would understand that a little bit of shallow could go a long way on a day like that?

My friends sandwiched me between them—they were both crutches and bodyguards—and we walked steadily down the center aisle to the empty front row at the base of the pulpit. That walk reminded me of the last minutes before an execution, the condemned prisoner taking her final walk from death row to the electric chair. I've never felt so many eyes on me, and I couldn't blame anyone for staring. How many times have I craned my neck at a funeral to see the widow's face—to get a glimpse of abject sorrow or to marvel at how she's holding it together? The spouse is the object of fascination; what must she be feeling? Will she break in front of us all? Didn't I always wonder how would I handle this if, God forbid, it were me?

It was me. My husband. My turn.

It was important that I speak at Doug's service. The room would be filled with people who'd known Doug for decades. Many had driven hundreds of miles across the country to attend the service. He and I had only been married for six and a half years, but I needed people to know that we were more than just a short chapter in his life. This would be my last moment to stand in front of others as Doug's wife. It was not lost on me that I'd been composing Doug's fortieth birthday toast for weeks, and now I was going to deliver it as a eulogy.

When the rabbi called me to the podium, Allison and Howard, who were sitting beside me, having arrived straight from Cantor's crisis center, reached over to squeeze my hand and tried not to cry. No one was ready to say good-bye to Doug, and this public confirmation of his death—no longer ambiguous or deniable—laid bare our already gaping wounds. I heard the room hush as I walked up the carpeted stairs to the lectern. Looking out at the congregation, I spotted a cluster of women who would soon deliver their own eulogies for husbands who'd died with mine in the North Tower. LaChanze Gooding, Calvin's widow, caught my eye as she sat soberly in the second row, her hands protectively wrapped around her pregnant belly. I saw Emily Terry, the widow of Andy Kates, who'd worked closely with Doug. His brother, Seth Kates, was also one of Doug's best friends from college and a regular golfing buddy. Susan Gurian, Doug Gurian's widow, sat nearby. Gurian grew up with my husband; they spent their childhood on the beaches and softball fields of Fire Island and lived in the same neighborhood for many years as young adults. Gurian had worked at Cantor, but left a few years earlier to join Radianz, another financial services firm. In a terrible twist of fate, he was attending a breakfast conference at Windows on the World at the top of the North Tower on September 11.

How was I going to speak to this room? I looked down at the detailed bullet points I'd composed the day before on blank sheets of computer paper while sprawled on my bedroom floor. Before I had written a word, I retrieved from under the bed a plastic, hinged box that contained dozens of greeting cards that Doug and I had exchanged and saved over the years. He marked every holiday, birthday, and anniversary with four or five eloquently worded missives hidden all over the house for me to discover. Doug didn't say a lot—he wasn't particularly chatty or careless with his words—but he wrote expressively and with passion. In each card he always included pet mantras such as "You're the one," "You make our life work," and "I love you madly." In one sitting, I read every card in the box, each one a heartbreaking testament to Doug's commitment as a devoted husband and father. If I was going to tumble into the truth in this speech, I would use Doug's own words as my guide. I also reread all of my cards to Doug, which didn't surprise me for the ardor they contained. I was almost infatuated with my husband, and the cards were the evidence. I always wrote "You're my hero" and concluded nearly each one with humble thanks for putting up with me.

I carried a few of our cards to the podium. I thought I might read excerpts to illustrate Doug's covert, playful side and how, after six and a half years of marriage, we were still reveling, even courting.

I thanked everyone for coming, admitted it was nearly impossible to stand in front of the packed room, and tried to sum up Doug's life in a few words. Before I could even get to Doug, though, I acknowledged the other new widows in the room and how unfathomable it was that so many were now gone. "God bless Cantor," I whispered into the microphone.

I didn't want to stand before everyone and describe Doug with a thesaurus-worthy litany of adjectives for noble, kind, and loving. He wasn't an image in the newspaper or a memory yet; he was still real, tangible, the big man with the hearty laugh whom everyone expected to walk through the door. Instead I shared anecdotes that I hoped would bring the man I adored into clear focus. After catching my breath, I told the congregation about our first weeks together. "Doug and I met on a blind date. He was intimidating at first; tall, handsome, and rather sure of himself. It took me a while to realize whether or not I liked him. Doug was powerful, he made a lot of decisions without consulting me, and, if you know me, I'm kind of used to being in control of things." People laughed. The tension broke slightly. I told everyone that Doug knew instinctively how to bring out the better, gentler aspects of my character, often reminding me, "I'm the best thing that ever happened to you."

I wanted to relax, to continue to tell breezy stories about our courtship, but I couldn't stop fidgeting. *Come home, Doug. I can't do this without you.* I retold the late-night-blizzard rescue story, when I knew that Doug was The One. "Our marriage was a lot like that snowy night," I said. "I loved the way Doug loved me. He put me first. He did this in little ways, day to day, like always ordering what I liked at restaurants because he knew I wouldn't like what I ordered. He was the same with the kids. Doug hated swimming, but would spend the entire day in the pool just because Julia wanted to jump to Daddy from the side, over and over again. I watched Doug with his aching knees and hulking six-foot-four-inch frame crawl through narrow metal cylinders and over tiny suspension bridges on swing sets to follow Michael's romps through the playground. Doug was committed; his happiness came from taking care of his family. And mine came from taking care of him."

My hands fluttered like two birds struggling to escape from a locked cage. I laced my fingers together and trapped my clasped hands tightly against my stomach. "Last Sunday was perfect. We spent the day in Central Park, riding bikes and scooters and having a picnic in Sheep Meadow. It was like the ending notes of a symphony, perfectly played."

I felt some inexplicable urgency to convey Doug as an effortless father and romantic husband, as if I couldn't let the crowd leave without knowing how singularly vast his absence would be for me. A lot of people died that day, of course, and I knew their losses reverberated with the same force as my husband's. But Doug was my loss, my unimaginable emptiness, and I felt some responsibility to paint him accurately. "This is who Doug was. He was more than you knew."

I lifted the two greeting cards from the podium and described our tradition of hiding multiple holiday cards "in drawers, the refrigerator, and under plates at restaurants. Doug didn't do anything small." I read part of the most recent Valentine's Day card I had written: "We fit together. Days and weeks can go by, and we sometimes just pass in the night. But then, we spend a day or two together alone, and I remember why we fell in love. Whether we're having a romantic dinner or sitting by the fire reading separate newspapers or schlepping around town doing errands, I am so thankful I'm doing it with you. You are the most wonderful husband. It all comes down to the little moments. . . . How did I get so lucky?"

My voice trembled, and it was difficult to keep from rambling. Suddenly, I recalled the last time I had spoken in front of a group. It was the previous spring—Doug and I were cochairing the annual benefit gala for the Jewish Community Center in Manhattan. The JCC was about to unveil its new building on Amsterdam Avenue, and we held the celebratory dinner at the Museum of Natural History. Doug teased me earlier that day that he looked forward to being my "arm candy" for the evening. I'd memorized my remarks and was to deliver them from a podium in the Whale Room, the museum's cavernous ocean exhibit. When I started my speech, my nerves caused me to race through the words. Doug was standing behind me and almost imperceptibly moved forward. I felt his hand gently touch the small of my back, and I immediately slowed down. He rested his hand there the entire time. My pulse returned to normal, I felt steady and even—I'll admit it, even a little powerful.

Now, standing in front of a thousand shell-shocked mourners pressed into the uncomfortable sanctuary of Stephen Wise Synagogue, I was starkly alone—Doug's soothing hand no longer on my back, no one there to steady me as I teetered.

I told the congregation with a voice wet with tears, "I feel very lucky. I had the love of my life. Please don't worry about me. Most people never get what I had. Doug loved me enough to last a lifetime. I don't need anything else. We'll be okay."

As I spoke those words scribbled on the crumpled paper in my hands, part of me was watching myself from a distance, and abruptly it hit me, I was done. Not just finished with the eulogy, but done permanently as a wife, a lover, a romantic half. It's crazy to say it, but to me, it felt simply factual: no wife ever loved her husband more than I loved Doug, and I would never do it again.

·····

A few days after the service, I got a call from Melanie, a former colleague from my single years. She and I spoke sporadically—careers, husbands, and babies have a way of winnowing the number of people with whom one keeps in touch. Also, Melanie was high-strung and a bit of a complainer, the type who'd receive a major promotion but fixate on the objectionable color of her new office furniture.

She told me she attended Doug's memorial service with her husband and couldn't stop thinking about it. Apparently, it had been an epiphany of sorts for her, and she wanted to tell me about it over lunch. For all I was concerned, she could have asked me to attend a city council budget meeting; I was just happy to have something to do for a few hours. We met at a local Malaysian restaurant on Columbus Avenue and settled into a booth by the window.

"You look so thin and tired," Melanie offered helpfully, as I ordered a cup of spicy lemongrass soup.

"Are you surprised?"

"Of course not. I was just saying." Her voice trailed off, and she adjusted her place setting.

We made small talk for a little while, but I could tell Melanie was distracted. She was twirling her hair the way she always did when she was anxious, and whenever I spoke, she nodded energetically, as if to nudge me more quickly to the conclusion. I was more than happy to yield the floor. In the days since Doug's death, I had become a modern version of the Ancient Mariner—I told and retold my story ad nauseam to whoever was at hand. I was already bored with my own voice, but helpless to stop. My poor friends—the daily winners of the widow lottery—listened patiently until I broke down, and the pathetic monologues would finally reach their inexorable conclusion.

Melanie finally jumped in. "Jennifer, I have to talk to you about the funeral. First, you were magnificent. Seriously, I couldn't believe you were able to stand in front of all those people and talk about Doug so calmly and with such humor. I don't think I could be that strong."

I always did a double take whenever anyone mentioned how strong I was or, worse, how only someone such as me could handle the tragic loss of a husband. A woman once actually said to me, "Oh, I could *never* survive if my husband died. I'm not strong like you, Jennifer." Are you kidding? I'm not strong like me either. I *am* you. I am that wife who clung to her husband, making him promise night after night that nothing would ever happen to him.

"Melanie, you would be surprised what you're capable of when you have no choice in the matter."

"Listen, I wanted to tell you that I listened to every beautiful word you said about Doug. And you know what? Of all the emotions I should have been feeling, all I felt was jealous."

I was dumbfounded. Jealous? How could anyone look at what our family lost and feel anything but sorrow or the need to send up a fervent prayer of "Please, God, not me"?

"Are you kidding? What are you talking about?" I retorted, a little too stridently.

Melanie straightened in her chair. "I mean, obviously, I felt bad for you and devastated that this happened. I've known you for so long my heart aches for you, Michael, and Julia. But, sitting at the service listening to you tell stories about your life with Doug, it was just so clear that he was your soul mate. I could feel him wrapped around you when you spoke, like even death couldn't sever that connection. And all I could think of was that I will never, ever have that."

I was aghast, but not surprised or even upset. I was actually somewhat amused. Leave it to Melanie to take me to lunch just to let me know how Doug's death was about her. "I just can't comprehend what you're saying. You've been married eight years to Kevin, who adores you. You have three healthy, stunning daughters. What don't you have?"

"I don't love Kevin like that," she answered quietly. "Your memorial service drove home for me that we'll never have your marriage, and I'm envious. I want what you had."

Melanie then proceeded to confess that she'd been having an affair with a tax attorney for the past six months. For the rest of lunch, she regaled me with the intimate details of trysts with her married paramour, including, to my mortification, dates, times, and hotels. After listening for an hour while Melanie described the sordid house of cards she'd constructed, my brain unspooled. I'd just lost a man whose only desire was to be home with his family, and there was Melanie, who, as a result of some narcissistic impulse, was willing to risk the destruction of hers. I couldn't fathom the disdain with which she viewed her blessed life. It took two hijacked airplanes to wreck my family, but Melanie was about to jettison hers in exchange for sweaty afternoons at the Marriott.

I should probably have lashed out, shook her out of her trance and made her realize she was on a collision course with herself that wouldn't end well. But, instead, I realized to my surprise that it actually wasn't so bad listening to someone else's fucked-up life for a change. At the least, Melanie killed two hours of my day, and I didn't have to say a word.

⋯⋯

Sometime during the week after Doug died, I took Michael for a walk to Amsterdam Avenue where Engine No. 40, Ladder No. 35, had its firehouse—a simple gray brick structure housed under a tall building on the corner of Sixty-Sixth Street. All twelve members of this brave company raced to the World Trade Center on September 11; only one survived. I hoped that Michael would feel less lonely knowing that he was not the only one who lost someone he loved. It was also something to do. I was thankful for anything that would fill up an hour.

One of the hardest parts of losing Doug was the utter silence at home. After I put the kids to bed, our empty apartment was disturbingly still. I had lost our language—the shorthand that Doug and I had only with each other. Our intimate vernacular, our nicknames, our silly word exchanges—all of the ways we knew each other without saying much were lost in an instant. Never again would Doug ask me to throw his socks "in the garbage" (hamper). Or, would I please turn on the "computer" (shower). To this day, I continue to talk "wrong" with the kids to try gently to inject Doug's presence into our everyday life.

Without my husband to share the minutiae of the day, it became unbearable to get through it. I especially dreaded the weekends. Doug was always home with us on the weekends. I couldn't get used to spending our family time without him. I looked forward to Mondays, when the city went back to work. At least during the weekdays I was already accustomed to Doug's not being around. I realized in an unbearable instant that everything that happened in our home would now happen in a vacuum. The joy of raising children was to see the experience reflected in my husband's eyes. Without him, the children and I were the proverbial trees in the forest, falling down without a sound. Who else besides Doug would listen enraptured to my retelling of Julia's giggly escapades at the sand table at school, or Michael's brilliant rendition of "You Are My Sunshine"? Only Doug could remind me that our day happened. How was I going to raise these beautiful children in silence, without Daddy to make us real?

Standing on the sidewalk outside the firehouse, I pointed out the piles of cards, candles, flowers, and toys that people had left to honor the men who died. I read Michael the list of names on a makeshift memorial. He asked me whether any of them were daddies. A young fireman with close-cropped blond hair and a baby face walked out of the firehouse. He asked Michael his name. When my eyes met his, tears instantly spilled over my cheeks as I sputtered somewhat incoherently that we had lost Michael's father. He touched my arm and told me that his brother, a member of this company, also died, and that he was temporarily working at this firehouse to honor his memory. I couldn't speak and turned away, sobs wracking my body. I heard him ask Michael if he'd like to come inside and have some cake. I waved my approval and paced the sidewalk until I could compose myself. When I caught up with my son inside, he was sitting before a table filled with cookies and cupcakes, contentedly holding a big plastic cup of milk.

"Random people drop off this stuff every day. I think everyone just wants to find a way to connect, to feel useful," the young fireman told me. I asked him how he was coping. He told me he was still in shock, but working at his brother's firehouse felt right. Michael asked to see the pumper truck, and together we made it through another afternoon.

·····

Sometimes getting through a day involved mundane chores that, under normal circumstances, would have been perfunctory and easy to accomplish. Going to the grocery store, buying stamps, keeping a dentist appointment—all became undertakings that required mental preparation and sometimes half a Xanax. Tasks requiring interactions in government buildings were especially fraught because I'd have to run the gauntlet of police officers, security personnel, and WE REMEMBER plaques hanging on every entrance. I felt small and weak in those places—unmasked without a place to hide. But the unexpected compassion from clerks and administrative officers on the front lines in these intimidating locations often astounded me. Less than a year after the attacks, I received a summons for jury duty. After listening to me explain that I was having "trouble" being downtown within blocks of the Trade Center, Kenny, a court clerk, took my hand and said, "Go home to your children. You've done enough for this city."

I also unraveled at the Department of Motor Vehicles when I had to transfer the title of our car from Doug's name to mine. Sitting on the hard bench waiting for my number to be called, I glanced at the manila folder in my hands containing the DMV's transfer forms. Beneath the papers were copies of my marriage license and Doug's death certificate, a blue-and-red document that listed his cause of death as "physical injuries (body not found)." I guess "murdered by terrorists" wasn't standard death-certificate language. To obtain a death certificate when a body is missing can be a time-consuming task through an unwieldy bureaucracy, but the city, in one of its many extraordinary acts of kindness, expedited the process for the Trade Center victims. Still, I couldn't get past the incongruity of seeing the death certificate next to our marriage license and quickly closed the folder.

When my number was called, I approached the counter and handed the materials to the tired young man waiting to process my request. We all know the negative stereotype of DMV workers, and I was anxious about how I would explain my situation. I shouldn't have worried. The minute he saw the death certificate, his eyes welled and he offered heartfelt condolences. Of course, that unleashed my own waterworks, which caused him to choke up more, and before we knew it, we were both a soggy mess. He quickly asked me to come around the counter so he could help me out of the sight of the rest of the DMV. He'd lost a cousin that day, too—every New Yorker was touched.

The ultimate New York moment, however, occurred at my local post office on Columbus Avenue nearly two months after the attacks. I went there to renew my son's passport. Though I had no intention of traveling out of the country ever again, I was nothing if not diligent, and an expiring passport required a timely renewal. As I stood in line with my death folder of official certificates, I noticed two firemen in full regalia standing right behind me. These guys must have been *there*, I thought to myself. They saw it firsthand. They lost friends because my husband was hopelessly trapped inside that inferno. I tried to reel myself away from these thoughts and focus on the task at hand. The woman behind the counter finally took my forms and Michael's old passport. "Where's the father?" she asked officiously when she saw Doug's name listed on the paper. My heart seized and the tears started as I passed her the death certificate. "He's deceased," I said shakily. "He died in the Trade Center." Before I knew what was happening, the two firemen surrounded me, one with his arm around my shoulder and the other pushed my paperwork to the surprised clerk. "She has everything in order, right? Can we just process her along quickly." The fireman with his arm around me asked if I was okay.

"Boy, you guys really know how to rescue someone," I joked weakly, trying to stop the mascara from blackening my entire face.

"We're so sorry for your loss. Can we help you at all?"

Still sniffling, I tried to make a quick exit. I was embarrassed for breaking down, especially in front of these men whose strength and bravery I couldn't fathom.

"No, I'm fine, really. Honestly, I don't have time to cry right now; I have an appointment with my therapist in fifteen minutes. I need to save this for her office."

"Ha, very funny. I'll tell you what, where's your appointment? We'll give you a ride."

"To the shrink? Absolutely not!" Now I was mortified. "The office is just a few blocks away on West End. I'm fine to get there by myself." By this time the two young men were smiling as they ushered me out of the post office. "No, ma'am, we insist. You're riding with us."

Imagine my shock when I walked (or should I say was nearly carried) out the door and saw an enormous fire engine parked at the curb with two more of New York's Bravest peering from the back window.

"Oh, no," I protested as I tried to stop my escorts from opening the cab door. "Really, guys, I'm fine. See? I'm not crying anymore."

"Climb aboard, ma'am. We're doing this."

I couldn't believe what was happening, but how could I refuse such a chivalrous offer from two dashing knights in bunker gear? I climbed into the truck and found myself tucked among four of the most sweet-faced, burly Irish guys I'd ever seen. I think there were two Patricks and a Christopher, but I can't remember exactly. They couldn't have been nicer or more empathetic. They asked whether my children and I were getting access to benefits, did I have a good support system, was the city reimbursing me for therapy bills. They asked where my husband was in the towers. When I said 105, they shook their heads. I feebly tried to tell them how much I appreciated their efforts and the heartrending sacrifices they'd made trying to save my husband and the others. They wouldn't let me speak, but I could see the raw pain behind their eyes. Maybe my accepting a ride was as much a distraction for them as it was for me. I will never forget it, nor will I forget my graceful exit from the cab when I missed the step and tumbled to the pavement in an ungainly heap. Thanks for the lift, boys.

······

You never know what's going to knock you down. You avoid listening to music or looking through photographs because you fear the inevitable dark wave. Family milestones loom in the distance (an anniversary, school conferences, birthdays), but at least for those you have time to prepare. The smaller ambushes come out of nowhere and leave you gasping. The day after the attacks, the sucker punch that leveled me came in the shape of a simple brown package delivered by the postman. It contained a box of twelve bespoke dress shirts by Turnbull & Asser. Doug would never wear them. He would never wear any shirt again. And I couldn't send them back because they were custom-made for a giant.

Staring at the useless box in my hands, the happy images of the day we ordered them during a recent trip to London lacerated the remainder of my fragile composure. Doug's frugality and aversion to shopping stopped at the doors of Turnbull & Asser's venerable shop on Jermyn Street in London. Most off-the-rack dress shirts didn't comfortably fit his bulky frame, causing him to surrender first reluctantly and later gleefully to the decadence of English custom shirt-making. Since he often traveled to London on business, Doug had become a regular at Turnbull & Asser and couldn't wait to take me there when we visited England over the summer.

I remembered Doug and I leisurely flipping through the fabric swatches under framed photographs of Prince Charles, Ronald Reagan, and other famous clients. Doug grimaced self-consciously when the associate took his measurements. "I'm the big man," he said, puffing up his chest proudly, "they're not used to the big men in England." Doug mentioned to the salesman that he'd purchased his first bespoke shirt there in 1982 when he spent his junior year of college at the London School of Economics. I'll never forget Doug's crimson face when the salesman found in the archives the nineteen-year-old manila envelope containing his more youthful measurements from that time.

I lay on the foyer floor clutching the brown box, knowing I could never bear to open it.

The simple act of checking my coat became a stark reminder that I was no longer married. I had to buy a larger dinner purse; the fashionably tiny clutches I used to carry couldn't accommodate the wallet, keys, and cell phone I now had to take everywhere because Doug wasn't carrying them in his jacket pocket for us. The morning of Doug's funeral, I put my lipstick on in front of the mirror in my foyer, closed the tube, and absently handed it behind me for Doug to pop into his coat pocket. Our private pas de deux was now a solo act.

I've always been independent. Upon graduating from law school, I moved to New York knowing just a handful of people. I rode the subway, paid my bills, and navigated the streets of New York like a native. After Doug and I were married, if I arrived ahead of him at a crowded party or restaurant, I had no trouble fending for myself. Imagine my surprise when I discovered, in the days and weeks following Doug's death, that I couldn't hail a taxi or meet a friend at a restaurant without crippling anxiety. A few days after the attacks, I had the doorman flag down a cab to take me to Howard and Allison's home to meet up with Doug's college friends who'd driven in from Boston to be with us. When I closed the car door, I felt as if I were suffocating, and it hit me— Doug would not be waiting at the other end of this ride. I called Allison and asked her to have someone meet me at the door to help me get out. She was standing on the sidewalk when my cab pulled to the curb.

Every night, good friends invited me for dinner or drinks to help break up the sickening, empty days I spent barely getting out of bed. Nights were the hardest. I was afraid to leave the apartment, but I just couldn't endure the lonely evening hours before bedtime when Doug was supposed to be home from the office. The dark, frozen apartment drove me out of the house so that, when I returned, I had just enough time to get in bed, take an Ambien, and wait for unconsciousness. And to minimize the panic of a public foray, I concocted a few rules.

First, I could only go to restaurants that Doug and I had never been to as a couple. (Eventually, the day came when I started to force myself to go everywhere we went to get the ache over with, so that I would never again have to say, "The last time I was here, Doug was with me.") Second rule: if I had to arrive at a restaurant alone, my companions had to promise and confirm by phone that they would be there before I arrived. Teeming restaurants rattled me because I could no longer find my tall, handsome husband above the crowd. Doug always knew where I was in a congested room. Now I hyperventilated at the thought of navigating the coat check. The last rule: have a predetermined escape route. At most dinners, there came a point in the night when I couldn't sit still a minute longer and had to flee. My good friends knew never to order coffee or dessert. Once, the Lutnicks invited me to have dinner in Westchester with our friends Stuart and Elise Fraser (Elise lost her only sibling, Eric Sand, in the attacks). The restaurant was an hour away from the city, so Allison and Howard brought a second car to carry me home the moment I felt the need to run.

·····

Grieving was like running a marathon in clogs. The finish line was miles away, I couldn't find momentum, and I was woefully ill-equipped. Being a high achiever was meaningless now; I was thunderstruck by my lack of progress as weeks turned to months. It wasn't that I was disorganized; I had everything in military order. But any emotional competence or clarity would evaporate as quickly as it came. I was just as lost on day sixty as I was on day one. I'd thought that once my apartment was cleared of bereft relatives and lasagnas—once my children had tidy calendars and car pools to play dates, ballet, and soccer—I could declare, "See, Doug, I did it. You made your point; I *can* manage solo. Enough already, come home."

Instead, after I completed each dreary task, all I could see ahead of me were days and decades without my husband. Weight fell off of me like new snow on a pitched roof. I looked skeletal, and not in a hot *Vogue*-magazine kind of way. Friends asked if I was eating. What was the point of lying? Of course I wasn't eating. I wasn't drinking, reading, or sleeping, either, so why eat? I did, however, shower, blow-dry my hair, and put on makeup every day. For what purpose, I had no idea.

My therapist said I was "agitated." What a great word. It reminded me of a restless mouse in one of those behavioral experiments, darting frantically and fruitlessly around a box, desperate to avoid the inevitable electric shock. My mind was never still. My brain was hyperaware of the monotonous details of my unfamiliar new life, but I retained nothing. My short-term memory couldn't withstand the constant assault of "I'm a widow, Doug is gone." In the middle of a sentence, I lost track of what I was saying. Forget about following other people's stories or television programs. I couldn't follow even the simple story lines of a *Friends* rerun. If I'd met someone in the few months preceding 9/11, I had no memory of it. Once, while wandering through a department store with Vicky, a woman approached who talked with me for ten minutes about Doug and how glad she was to see me looking so put together. "Who was that?" I asked Vicky when the woman walked away. "I don't know. I thought you knew her," she replied. What was wrong with my brain?

I warned friends not to tell me anything in confidence. Whatever popped into my brain flew off my tongue without censor. I was an unpredictable geyser of unfiltered non sequiturs and caustic one-liners. My poor mother absorbed the brunt of many of these verbal surges. One night, when I returned from dinner, she was sitting in the living room waiting for me as if I were a teenager returning after curfew. I exploded at her, "Don't you dare wait up or ask me where I've been tonight or any night. I did not suddenly become sixteen again because Doug died. You don't get a do-over. You're here to help with the kids, not raise me again." God bless my mother. It's amazing she didn't get on the first train back to Massachusetts. I asked my friends to grant me a widow's waiver. I needed a standing get-out-of-jail-free card until my frontal cortex eventually reattached itself.

·····

The children's school reopened two days after the attacks. I decided that I was strong enough to accompany my not-yet-three-year-old daughter alone to her first day. (Panic attacks had a way of coming on unexpectedly—in the grocery store, in a dentist's chair—but it was Julia's first day, and I didn't want someone else to fill my role.) Without considering the ramifications of going to a public place so soon, I was surprised when, upon entering the synagogue, the throngs of parents and children parted like the Red Sea. No one expected to see me. I lifted Julia into my arms, buried my face in her sweet neck, and walked to her classroom. The teacher asked the parents to sit in a row of tiny chairs while the children independently explored the room. Julia established herself at the water table and began pouring water over a plastic windmill. A plump, pale-faced woman with cascades of dirty-blond curls leaned over to me and whispered, "I can't believe it." I smiled weakly, "I know. It's so hard to see this without Doug." Her reply? "Umm, yeah, that is something. But, I was, uh, referring to the fact that I can't believe my son is separating from me."

The mothers at the preschool decided to take turns delivering biweekly dinners to my family during the fall semester. Everyone wanted to help someone affected by the attacks, and I was within reach. At first I didn't want to accept; I was afraid of being a pathetic charity case—the poor widow who couldn't feed her own children. But the simple reality was that the help was welcome and the moms, mercifully, kind and discreet. Most dinners arrived anonymously in disposable containers, which relieved me of having to return pots and dishes the next day at school like used soda bottles at a recycling center. None of the families ever asked to be acknowledged, and I was deeply touched by everyone's generous efforts to help me reacclimate to a regular routine. The dinners ran smoothly, except when it was Diane's turn. Every school has a Diane. You know the type—she's the mother who thinks she runs every committee, breezily dispenses unsolicited parenting advice, and never lets anyone forget she works full-time.

A sturdy woman with thick, unruly black hair and a force-ful gait, Diane approached me at morning drop-off to discuss "logistics" for her meal. She informed me that she would deliver dinner in the morning because "You know, I work full-time and will have to make it after work the night before if I'm ever going to get it to you on time."

I was humiliated. "Oh, Diane, please don't worry. I have plenty of food. You don't have to do this at all."

"Of course I'm going to bring you dinner. I signed up, it's my turn. It's just that I work and need to deliver it in the morning."

"It's okay, Diane. It's very kind of you to do this. It is really not necessary."

"Well, it's fine. And, you're going to love it. By the way, you can return the bowl at school the next day."

Diane sent a covered dish of beef and broccoli. At drop-off the next day, I saw her hovering outside the classroom by the kids' cubbies. Clearly, she was waiting for me.

"So, did you like it? Didja?"

I smiled humbly and gave her the clean bowl. "Thank you. It was very nice. Thank you for thinking of us." I turned to help Julia hang her pink jacket in her cubby, which was overflowing with paintings and collages that I should have taken home weeks ago.

"You know, it's the funniest story," Diane started, as Julia scampered into her classroom. "I had to leave work early just to make you dinner, and while I was cooking, my husband walks in, sniffs the air, and says, 'You're making that beef and broccoli that we love! I'm so excited you're making dinner.' Can you believe, Jennifer? I was so busy making your family dinner that I forgot to make *my family* dinner!"

To be fair, she wasn't the first or last to lob a mind-boggling bon mot my way during that awful time. I didn't mind and even welcomed most of the awkward things people said because they were said with such sincerity and good intentions. I appreciated every attempt to connect, to empathize or let me know my family was in someone's thoughts. However, I have to admit there were some beauties. "How does it feel to be famous?" said one preschool mom at drop-off, as she draped an unwelcome arm around my shoulder with a toothy smile. "Were you close to your husband?" was another thoughtful inquiry. "I heard that young children who lose their fathers can suffer real psychological damage during their developmental years." Gee, I wish someone had warned me before I decided to lose my husband. It seemed like such a good idea at the time . . .

And it didn't stop there. About eight weeks after the attacks I was having dinner with Pam, and her friend Debbie, at Park, a trendy, cavernous lounge on West Eighteenth Street. Just as our drinks arrived, Debbie matter-of-factly posited, "When you're in a bar, you *must* be looking around at all the single guys. It's kind of exciting to think about dating again, right?" Pam turned white. "I'm married," I replied bluntly, not bothering to conceal my contempt for her tactless inquiry.

However, therein lay the problem: I *wasn't* married, but I also wasn't single. Going out to dinner with a group of single girlfriends—friends who'd never been married—depressed me. I loved my friends, but was I really going to be relegated to a life of girls' nights out and profile updates on JDate and Match.com just because Doug had died? The mere thought of blind dates gave me hives. After loving Doug for so long, how could I possibly sit across from some earnest investment banker and blithely engage in the enervating "What are you looking for in a mate?" first-date conversation?

Once, I inadvertently admitted to a new acquaintance that

nights were the most difficult time because Doug didn't come home. "Oh, you should relish that time," she offered brightly. "I love it when my husband goes away for a few days, and I get to have the bed to myself." I know, my head also spun in disbelief that anyone could be so truly obtuse, but sometimes the most thought-less comments were the most welcome. My favorite came in early November when Vicky and her husband, David, invited me to dinner at a neighborhood Italian restaurant with another couple I didn't know apart from having met them briefly at the JCC. I liked them instantly, and the five of us immediately settled into animated discussions ranging from the stock market to raising chil-dren in Manhattan to plastic surgery. It was so nice to have that little respite—to sit with married couples and just have a normal night out was a rare gift. As the evening wore on and the wine flowed, our tongues loosened, and the laughter emanating from our table probably irked a few of the diners in the small restaurant.

Suddenly, the husband turned to me and said, "You know, Jen-nifer, you're going to get laid again."

The table went silent. Maybe it was the wine or that he didn't know me well, but for some reason it was the funniest thing I'd ever heard. I know it sounds ridiculous, but that's the magic of timing and a smooth delivery from an audaciously charming din-ner companion. I tried to look shocked like everyone else, but it was difficult to keep a straight face. His wife was shaking her head, and Vicky looked as if she were about to dive under the table. My new friend, unconcerned, pressed on, "Jennifer, seri-ously, I know. It's gonna happen."

"Honey," his wife hissed. "That's enough!"

"What's wrong with what I said? It's true. She's not going to spend the rest of her life celibate."

At that point I couldn't suppress it in any longer. I started to laugh so hard tears rolled down my cheeks, and the entire table followed suit.

"My friend, I appreciate your confidence," I said between convulsions. "You're a riot. But, honestly, it's not in the cards. I'm fine as I am."

"Mark my words, Jen. I know you're not thinking about it right now and probably not for a long time, but it isn't over for you. Not by a long shot."

⋯⋯

After Doug's memorial, I didn't go out much during the day unless I was attending a funeral. The services started to accumulate quickly—there were several Cantor services each week for several months. We were in many ways the epicenter of 9/11 having lost so many people. Howard decided early on that Cantor should organize its own memorial for the families of its 658 dead employees. It would be a rare private moment—one that Cantor would repeat every year on the anniversary for ten years—that enabled family members to touch and comfort one another. It also allowed Howard to reach more people, to let his employees' families see that he was one of them, mourning the loss of his brother, close friends, and too many coworkers.

On October 1, a cool, drizzly morning, Cantor held an enormous memorial service that spilled over Central Park's Rumsey Playfield, home to SummerStage. From outside the iron gates, the large white tents, flag-draped stage, and sea of white folding chairs gave the impression of a college graduation. Once inside, however, the sight of hundreds of names running along the makeshift walls of auxiliary tents and the many tables holding three-tiered trays of Kleenex packs quickly dispelled any sense of celebration. Four thousand people attended the service. Jayme and Scott steered me through the crowd to the foot of the stage, where Allison was waiting to show us to our seats next to hers in the front row. I hadn't been surrounded by so many people since Doug's funeral. I felt disoriented, lost among the dark suits and red-rimmed eyes. There were dozens of quick embraces with wives of Doug's colleagues. We smiled and asked reflexively, "How are you?" A teary nod and slight shrug of the shoulders provided the only practical answer. We hadn't yet developed a vocabulary to manage these greetings.

I saw Allison at the front, hugging family members and valiantly trying to make contact with each person vying for her attention. My first impulse was to run to her side, to lend support as I always did at Cantor functions. Instead, I stayed frozen, my heels sinking into the grass. Amid the throng of pallid faces it finally dawned on me that I wasn't a Cantor wife anymore. I wasn't here to help host the firm's holiday party or fund-raiser. Cantor was hosting me, merely one of the many families asked to gather to mourn collectively the loss of everyone we knew.

Allison's older brother, Gary Lambert, walked over. Gary is a darkly handsome, powerfully built man who spent the last Sunday before the attacks with Allison's family and mine in Central Park, teaching the kids to ride bicycles and buying rainbow Popsicles from the ice cream cart. Gary engulfed me in an enormous bear hug. I stiffened automatically and patted his arm. Gary asked me why I wouldn't hug back. I didn't have an answer, but smiled weakly. In truth, every time someone touched me it threatened to fracture the protective shell I'd constructed and needed to navigate public outings. I couldn't both honestly hug someone like Gary and also stay composed and focused. It was one or the other.

Allison looked up from the horde of people surrounding her. Seeing me, she gently excused herself from her conversation and wrapped her arms around me. Again, I recoiled. I wanted to hug her, to bury my face in her shoulder or affirm that we—she and I—were still intact. But I'd shorted out. Too many people were clamoring for her attention, and I just couldn't be one of them right now. I wanted my old job back. I wanted to be the person I used to be, propping up, pitching in. But Doug was dead, the door was closed, and I didn't belong here anymore. Allison was worried, I saw it in her eyes, but I was helpless to reassure her. She asked a little sharply why I wouldn't hug her. I squeezed her hand and said, "It's okay. I just need to sit."

We took our seats, and the service began. The Boys Choir of Harlem stood on risers across the stage. I couldn't believe what unfolded in front of me. Stuart Fraser, Howard and Doug's openhearted, effusive partner and nephew of the wife of Cantor's founder, stood on the stage colorless, weighed down as he opened the ceremony with a few halting words. Stuart survived because he'd had the good fortune to be at home that deadly morning preparing for a meeting in Westchester. A solemn procession of religious leaders, new widows, and politicians addressed the crowd. Judy Collins sang "America the Beautiful" in a voice almost ghostly and spare. At one point Mayor Giuliani and Howard were holding hands, swaying awkwardly to the Boys Choir's "We Shall Overcome." At that very moment, I felt two hands on my shoulders and turned around. Sarah Ferguson, the Duchess of York, was giving me a sympathetic back rub. Where the hell was I? Clearly, down the rabbit hole. I quickly stifled the inappropriate laugh threatening to shatter the solemnity and bent over, pretending to look for my purse lying on the grass between the chairs. It was all too surreal to take in. Allison turned to me in alarm, thinking I'd collapsed in tears. "Are you all right? What is it?" she asked, touching my head to draw my eyes to hers. She was confused that I seemed "off" somehow, that I hadn't allowed her to comfort me, that I said so little. I was infuriated with myself. I could chuckle at Giuliani's marked lack of rhythm, yet not be able to muster a real hug for my best friend? It didn't make sense. Yes, I admit, it was impossible to see myself next to Allison without the life I was supposed to be living with Doug. But, so what? She wanted to be there for me, not as the wife of Cantor's chairman, but as my best friend, the person who knew me better than anyone else. I had to get a handle on my grief if we were ever going to find our way back to even a semblance of what we had. We needed each other, and besides, I knew she had to be thinking the same thing I was about the absurd display unfolding before us.

"I just don't think I can watch any more of this Rudy and Howard 'Hands Across America' moment. They're starting to look like a cute couple—you may have to do something about it."

Allison put her hand over her mouth to suppress a giggle. Relief washed over her face. "You crack me up," she said, tipping her head to touch mine.

"I'm trying, Allison," I said, feeling my chest start to tighten. "Please be patient with me."

"Always. I just want to help."

"I know. I love you. It's just going to take time."

The Boys Choir finished the song, and we turned together to watch the surviving Cantor employees line up before two microphones to read the names of the dead.

3

They say nothing looks as good as thin feels, but after several weeks on a widow's diet of green grapes, chicken broth, and minimal sleep, I'd beg to differ. I didn't look good at all, not that I cared about my appearance, but my sunken eyes and "crack addict" arms never failed to shock me. My clothes hung limply from the wire hanger that had become my body.

My favorite sales assistant, Tony Curtis, called me one afternoon from the Jeffrey New York store in the trendy Meatpacking District. Unlike his namesake, this Tony Curtis was a rail-thin, African-American man from Georgia with an outrageous wardrobe, Cheshire-cat smile, and unnatural obsession with all things Patti LaBelle. Tony's wickedly fabulous demeanor masked a deep sensitivity. Everyone loved him. Shopping with Tony didn't necessarily involve buying anything; more often than not we spent our time gabbing on the sofa amid the decadent shoe displays or sneaking away for a quick lunch at Markt on Fourteenth Street. Tony was one of the first people to call after the

attacks. Later, when he heard from a friend that I looked ema-
ciated, he arrived at my door unannounced with Jeffrey's best
seamstress to take in the waists on all of my trousers, regardless
of where I bought the clothes. He refused to charge me. I still
have the belt that he gave me during that time—I think it fits
my twelve-year-old daughter.

The smallest gesture could make the biggest difference. For
me, it was the red Valentino dinner bag. When the summer ends,
certain New York women begin planning their fall calendar of
social events, charity galas, and luncheons. While they filled their
date books and mapped their wardrobes, I calculated the number
of funerals, wakes, and shivahs I'd be attending in the next three
months. Clearly, the new scarlet gown I'd bought for my sister's
wedding would have to take a sabbatical for the foreseeable
future. Basic black and conservative pumps became my uniform
for the season. I didn't own many clothes suitable for mourning.
Tony came to my rescue. He commandeered a dressing room
in the back of Jeffrey's and convinced me to come downtown.
"Honey, you need to come see Tony," he drawled over the phone
in his comforting Southern-belle accent. "It will do you good to
get out of the house. I promise I will take care of you. No one will
see your bony ass but me."

He met me at the store's huge glass doors and quickly escorted
me up the stairs, past the brightly lit makeup counters, glass cases
of delicate jewelry, and racks of the latest "it" accessories. He led
me through multitiered displays of sparkly stilettos and fine
leather boots to a small doorway just before the clothing section
and cocooned me in a white, heavily curtained dressing room.
How many times did Tony and I giggle and dish in this plush
little oasis? How many times did Doug sit in this chair holding
my bag and jacket while I tried on various ensembles (including

that now abandoned red gown) and vamped for his approval? Buying was never the goal of these outings with Doug. Flirting with him in the dressing room was.

On this day, however, my depleted frame barely filled Doug's corner chair. Tony sat at my feet holding my hand, and we just rested there quietly for a long time. He had gathered a small selection of conservative, simple pieces to get me through the services and sympathy calls. I felt like Dorothy in reverse: the staid, black-and-ivory garments glared at me—you're not in Oz anymore. Tony helped me try on a dark suit, black trousers, and a few modest blouses. He summoned the seamstress, and while waiting for her to arrive, I slumped into my chair and started to cry. "I shouldn't be here, Tony. I don't think I can do this." Suddenly, a young sales associate from accessories burst into the dressing room brandishing a stack of shoe boxes and a few purses. "Thought you might like to take a look at the new collection while you're here," he chirped brightly. I shook my head rapidly: "No, please no." Tony swiftly lunged at the now frozen man to hustle him out of the room. "Get out, please. She doesn't want to look at any of this." I glanced up at the poor associate shrinking from Tony's charge and noticed a bright red Valentino bag dangling from his finger. Through my tears I heard myself blurt out, "Um, wait, that red bag is kind of nice."

Tony stopped instantly and wheeled around to me. "You like this? Do you want to look at it?"

"No . . . yes. I don't know." Tony snatched the purse from the hapless associate and dismissed him through the curtain.

The small, rectangular, red suede handbag had a thin leather strap. Its metal clasp was shaped in the famous *V*-in-a-circle logo. In my previous life, I might have bought that beautiful jewel in a heartbeat. Now its ruby radiance chided, "You are no longer you."

Yet something inside my anesthetized body stirred at the sight of the cheerful color.

The incongruity of bawling my eyes out and simultaneously noticing a red Valentino bag was not lost on Tony. He giggled, "Honey, Jennifer has not left the building. Thank the Lord, you're still in there somewhere." He asked me if I wanted it. I said I couldn't spend money on something so frivolous. Tony leaned over and said quietly, "You should take it. You'll carry it one day when you're happy again."

"I can't."

"Shhhh, don't tell anyone. I'm giving you the widow's discount—fifty percent off."

I pulled out my AmEx.

I still have Tony's purse. It sits at the back of a top shelf in my closet wrapped in tissue. I haven't carried it in many years (and probably only used it twice), but I look at it from time to time when I need to remind myself that despair isn't permanent. Tony showed me that hope always exists, even in the shape of a silly designer indulgence.

Tony died in 2009 after a long, painful battle with cancer. During my last conversation with him, we reminisced about that day in the dressing room. He asked me whether I still had our Valentino. Tony, my friend, I'm holding it as I type.

·····

I decided to do an interview with Connie Chung three days after the attacks. A close friend was a senior producer for ABC News and asked if I would be willing to personalize the loss on television. A newly minted widow was certainly a "get" for any news organization at that early date, and I trusted that my friend

would treat my story properly. I agreed to participate in her segment because I desperately needed to speak about my husband,
remove him from the statistics, and make his life real, specific, and
consequential. Every day took him further away from me, and I
feared his memory would become just a collection of anecdotes
and frozen snapshots in an album. I also needed my children to
know that Daddy loved them and would never willingly leave
them. I once read somewhere that, when a parent dies, children
frequently believe the deceased parent intentionally abandoned
them. It crushed me to think that our children would ever doubt
Daddy's inability to survive. Michael had already shared several
theories about whether Daddy could have escaped the building if
he had found the stairs or jumped from a lower floor. In a panic,
I thought that having a recorded broadcast days after the attacks
of my telling the kids about Daddy's love for them would prove
that Daddy tried his best to come home.

ABC asked me to provide photographs of Doug and our family to run with the segment. I arrived at the studio clutching
several photos, still in frames, which I'd pulled off the wall in my
hallway. Chung greeted me outside her office. The minute I saw
her, I regretted my decision to participate. She approached me
with her heavily made-up face tilted to one side and a closed-
mouth smile that oozed practiced sympathy. God, I hated the
head tilt. It made me feel like a three-legged dog. Worse, the
head tilt was usually accompanied by the tilter's obligatory "How
are we doing today?" and the abject fear that I might actually
answer the question truthfully. I stiffly accepted Chung's awkward embrace, and she led me to two hard chairs positioned
under television lights. I attached a microphone to my blue shirt,
and the camera rolled. I felt like the proverbial deer in headlights,
but Chung competently led me through the interview. She asked

several questions about The Day. She wanted to know where I was when I heard about the attacks and did anyone talk to Doug. Indeed, Joe Gardner had, and Doug calmly told him that they were trying to get everyone out of the building. Chung then asked when was the moment I accepted that Doug had perished. "When I saw the building collapse, I felt his presence leave me," I answered. Part of me felt empowered knowing that, through this piece, my children might understand that Daddy was so important even the news wanted to put his picture on television. But, sitting in that chair, I realized I had no control how my words would be edited and interpreted. My children might never watch this, but I now had to live with my willingness to put a public face on the nightmare.

The questions continued. Chung asked me whether Howard Lutnick was treating the families fairly. I told her that Howard was a hero and deserved full support from the media and the city for all the heart-wrenching work he and his partners were doing on our behalf. ABC never aired this part of the interview. Howard had received unfairly negative press for ceasing to issue paychecks to deceased employees' families a week after the attacks. The media didn't understand that Howard wanted to ensure that Cantor could financially support the families for years and not just for a few weeks. Indeed, he and his partners distributed 25 percent of Cantor's profits to the families for five years, and two days after the attacks, they established the Cantor Fitzgerald Relief Fund to assist family members of the 658 employees who perished. Fully underwritten by Cantor and valiantly run by Edie Lutnick, Howard's sister, the fund provided financial support such as ten years of free health care for spouses and their children, legal representation before the federal Victim Compensation Board, and an invaluable website that served as a clearinghouse of information about federal, state, and private resources available for 9/11 victims. Unlike the other companies in the World Trade Center that cut off financial and most other assistance by the end of 2001, Cantor continues to this day to provide support services to its deceased employees' families. But it seemed to me that Chung wasn't interested in shining a positive light on Howard or Cantor. In a later interview, she cast Howard as a villain—a striving, greedy power broker who cared more for the bottom line than the employees who died working for him. It was shameless, biased, and utterly false.

As our conversation came to a close, Chung gave me the opportunity to "tell the world" anything I wanted to say. The tears, which had remained locked in my eyes up to that point, spilled over as I explained, "I just want my children to know that Daddy didn't leave because he wanted to. He was taken. It wasn't his fault, and it wasn't their fault. Daddy loved them." The interview ended. We stood up and removed the microphones. Chung flashed me a bright white smile and said, "Amazing. How is it that you can cry and your eye makeup doesn't smudge?"

My interview ran that night on the ABC evening news with Peter Jennings. The segment prompted several welcome phone calls and e-mails from college friends and aquaintances across the country wanting to offer condolences and reconnect. But, the interview also proved once again that, because of the magnitude of 9/11, my life was mere grist for the mill of public opinion. The overeager preschool mom who gushed, "How does it feel to be famous?" delivered those memorable words to me the morning after the broadcast. Several weeks later, I was walking with Michael into a sports club on Columbus Avenue for his karate class when I suddenly heard my voice coming from the café's television set saying, "I felt his presence leave me." Holding tightly to my son's hand, we watched Oprah Winfrey conclude her "Getting in Touch with Your Spirit" segment with portions of my ABC interview. I've always admired Oprah, but couldn't I have been in the studio audience for her "Favorite Things" extravaganza instead? The media's repackaging of 9/11 into chopped and easily accessible bits of voyeurism had begun. And I had now played my part.

· · · · ·

In the winter, I received a group e-mail from Allison. It was addressed to the wives of Cantor Fitzgerald's executives who died that day. I think I counted ten of us, all women I knew from family picnics, holiday parties, and dinners—all women whose lives imploded in one terrible instant. I was especially close with two of them: LaChanze, who'd given birth to her daughter, Zaya, a little over a month after the attacks, and Erin Richards, the petite widow of Greg Richards, a young rising star at Cantor and father of their two-year-old son, Asher. Since the attacks, I'd talked regularly with Erin and LaChanze; we were each other's mirror, the only other people on earth who could understand how the simple act of bathing a child, seeing a poster of the Twin Towers at the post office, or calling the gym to cancel our husband's membership could paralyze us for three days. My friendships with each of them developed into deep dependence. All of us were lonely, bored, and terrified.

Early on, Allison conceived of and organized support groups in three states for each of the various "categories" of family members: spouses, fiancées, new mothers, parents, and siblings. Run by trained psychologists and trauma specialists, the groups were held in New York, Connecticut, and New Jersey, in areas where

Cantor families were concentrated. These gatherings became lifelines for people, thanks to Allison. She wanted every single family member to have a refuge, a guide.

I sat at my desk reading her invitation to reunite the executive wives for a dinner at the Lenox Room, a local restaurant on the Upper East Side. I instantly squirmed in my seat. Of course it made perfect sense to gather this particular group of women together. We'd all become friends through our husbands' work—we looked forward to seeing one another whether at a Cantor charity event or a Friday night dinner on Long Island. With the deaths of our husbands, Allison recognized that our only opportunities to be in the same room again might be limited to memorial services. She and Howard didn't want to disconnect from us or let us fall away from one another as we rebuilt our decimated lives. Allison's dinner would give our extended family a chance to spend real time together and perhaps provide all of us with a little comfort in knowing we weren't grieving alone.

But why did this invitation feel like a summons? I started to panic at the thought of having to assemble with my "category" at a dead husbands' dinner. (Allison hated when I said that—I admit it's insensitive, but sometimes grossly inappropriate humor allowed me to reduce a tragic feast into a digestible bite.) Of course, Allison only had the best intentions. But even the best intentions sometimes rubbed me the wrong way. I resisted any organized gathering that related to 9/11. Doug's death was already so nauseatingly public, part of CNN montages, a branded American moment of patriotism and resilience that spawned countless book contracts, television ratings, political careers, documentaries, and cheesy memorabilia. In just a few months, the catastrophic loss of individuals was sound bites and schmaltz—recovered pieces of rubble and office papers, flag pins and iconic photographs, glitzy televised fund-raisers and replayed videos of terrified office workers fleeing from plummeting debris. A sound track was already composed and playing underneath this story, and I didn't want to play my part in the movie.

I know the country mourned with us, but I couldn't bring myself to mark Doug's death on anyone else's schedule. I wanted to look at Doug's loss only when I, alone, felt I needed to. So, I never joined a support group. I know that many women felt soothed and bolstered by these gatherings and sharing their stories. I just felt stripped bare, diminished. Yes, I had a shrink—a straight-talking, maternal woman who encouraged me to say the worst and feel the saddest. That personal hour each Thursday, venting to my captive, well-paid psychiatrist, became sacred to me. Doug's loss was in a locked box, to be shared only with those I trusted or paid. I was grateful to live in a city that allowed total anonymity. In the suburbs, everyone knows everybody—you can't go to Starbucks or have an unfamiliar car in your driveway without the neighbors buzzing. In the city, I could move openly, hiding my Scarlet *W* behind a faux smile and freshly made-up face. Allison's invitation destabilized the artifice.

I called LaChanze. "Are you going?"

"I am if you are."

"I think we have to go. Allison really wants to get everyone together. We need to be there."

I called Erin. "Are you going?"

"Only if you are."

"Erin, why does this make me feel so put upon and uncomfortable? Why can't I see it the way Allison does, as a nice opportunity to be together?"

"Because it isn't like any dinner you've ever had with her. Our lives are upside down, and I think you're worried how it will feel to watch her host these women whose one thing in common is that their deceased husbands worked for Cantor."

Okay, I was being neurotic, but Doug's loss did that to me. I wasn't expecting the invitation, and it threw me. I wasn't good with surprises anymore (not that anyone ever accused me of being spontaneous and laid-back). At the same time, I beat myself up for being ungenerous. Allison was hurting, too—it wasn't easy for her to be surrounded by unremitting grief. She and Howard would have been well within their rights to close Cantor, pack up their family, and move to a ranch in Montana. But they didn't. They stayed.

"We're going, right?" I asked Erin.

"I'll see you there."

I walked into the Lenox Room on Third Avenue. It was a dimly lit neighborhood spot with an upholstered lounge area and candlelit tables. The hostess directed me to the far end of the room, where a long table was set, and a few women had trickled in. Among them I spotted Eileen Varacchi. Her husband, Fred, had been her high school sweetheart and president of eSpeed (Cantor's electronic bond exchange). Doug recruited Fred and worked closely with him to build the new division. I believe they were together when the towers collapsed. I also saw Rise Goldflam, whose husband, Jeff, was the CFO of Cantor. Doug and I had just enjoyed our first nonwork-related dinner with them about two weeks prior to 9/11. We'd clicked as couples; I remember laughing at their amusing horror stories about raising teenagers. The other women started to arrive, each looking strangely beautiful and put together. True, each of us had lost significant weight, but some color had started to return. One could easily have mistaken this scene as a girls'-night-out birthday dinner, though a closer look would have revealed an awkward bunch.

Allison was standing at the head of the table affectionately greeting each of us. As always, she looked striking in her dark suit with a flag pin attached to her lapel. I gave Allison a long hug and thanked her for putting this together. She was relieved and happy about the turnout and couldn't wait to see everyone: "I really miss our friends. It's lonely without them." Allison's heart was in the right place, and I wanted to support her efforts. I put on my game face and entered the room. A server took drink orders as we milled around, sipping wine, eating canapés off tiered trays, and quietly reassuring one another: "You look so well." I started to get my bearings and silently berated myself for overreacting to the invitation. It wasn't the first time that the dread of anticipation was worse than the reality. This had all the makings to be a pleasant, even welcome evening.

Then I saw Elise Fraser and Robin Shanus enter the room. Their presence caught me off guard. What were *they* doing at a widows' dinner? Elise was married to Stuart Fraser, Doug's great friend and the senior partner who had stayed in Westchester on the morning of September 11. Robin was married to Stephen Merkel, Cantor's general counsel, who miraculously survived the attacks when he stepped off the North Tower's elevator into the lobby at nearly the exact moment one of the planes struck the building. I adored Robin and Elise; the Lutnicks, Frasers, Merkels, and Gardners were a regular foursome. In our family room, I had a framed photograph of the four couples at Le Bernardin, celebrating the 1996 court victory that confirmed Howard as Bernie Cantor's successor after a very public, but ultimately unsuccessful, challenge by Bernie's wife. That contentious face-off had brought our husbands closer and forged a permanent bond among the wives. But they were still married, their families still intact; I wasn't. They hadn't had to explain to their children that Daddy wasn't coming home or had to put their husbands' toothbrushes into a Ziploc bag for DNA testing. So, why were they here? And why was I so upset to see my two dear friends whom I spoke to nearly every day?

I took a sip of wine and tried to understand why Allison included them. Obviously, Elise and Robin missed their spirited circle as much as Allison did. But in this sober room, so soon after the attacks, the gap between the haves and have-nots was unmistakable. I couldn't absorb the dissonance.

I found Erin and directed her toward the table. "You have to sit with me."

Erin knew exactly what was bothering me. She felt it, too, but neither of us was proud of how we reacted to the sight of two women we loved and would have been thrilled to see under any other circumstance. Allison invited everyone to be seated. Erin and I huddled at one end of the softly lit table. Allison sat at the far end, and Elise and Robin sat separately among us. It was an odd tableau. I tried to look engaged in conversation with Erin. We reminisced about the last time we'd seen each other, in Palm Beach during the recent winter school break. We met for lunch at Ta-boo restaurant on Worth Avenue, the posh strip of designer boutiques. We didn't shop. Instead, at a little café table by a front window that looked at the street, we spent two hours as any newly widowed mothers would, swapping tales of psychiatrists, antidepressants and single parenting. Both of us were wobbly, but also, amazingly, not in a fetal position anymore. I think we surprised ourselves when we agreed that, somehow, we were going to survive this.

Erin and I talked straight through dinner, frequently engaging two other women who were seated with us. Once the conversations fell into a comfortable groove, I was content to sit there for the rest of the night. It seemed that all of the women at the table had nestled into relaxed exchanges with immediate neighbors. It was safer that way, less exposed. As the server cleared the dinner plates and took dessert orders, I felt a tap on my shoulder. Allison.

"Jen, will you switch seats with me? I'd like to have a chance to talk with this side of the table during dessert."

As I've said before, you never know what's going to knock you down. First it was the box of bespoke shirts, and now an innocuous request from my best friend to change seats. Prior to 9/11, switching seats was a normal part of our dinnertime choreography. Allison and I often sat at separate tables during large Cantor dinners or charity events and exchanged seats during dessert to visit with all of the guests. The husbands did, too. Changing places was never an issue before, but now it felt cruel and unfair. At the Lenox Room safely seated with "my kind," I felt composed, handling my grief with either the same clumsiness or aplomb as everyone else. But the second I felt I was supposed to fulfill a role I'd easily played a thousand times before, I fell apart. I wasn't the graceful cohost anymore. That Jennifer evaporated when Doug didn't come home. I couldn't table-hop; I almost couldn't get out of the cab that night. I was just starting to feel at ease, and now I could barely breathe. Why couldn't she have asked someone else?

"Sure," I said, and reached for my purse.

I stood up, a little unsteadily, and looked at Erin. Only she saw the color drain from my face, but could say nothing. I walked to Allison's abandoned seat and sat down, fiddled with a spoon, carving circles on the tablecloth. It wasn't Allison's fault, but I faulted her. And then faulted myself for faulting her. I realized my best friend had overestimated me—she thought I was still, despite it all, the competent, resilient, witty Jennifer she'd always known. Which I appreciated, but couldn't sustain. Of course she knew I'd unraveled, but not how far; probably because I hadn't fully let her find out.

Coffee was served, and Howard suddenly appeared at the table, still in his suit from the office. With a big smile, he greeted his deceased partners' wives,

"Hello, everyone. I just wanted to come by and see you before you left."

He circled the table, a big hug for each of us. When he got to Allison, he kissed her warmly and brushed a strand of hair off her face. That's how a husband greets his wife, I thought. Doug would have kissed me hello just like that.

Allison and Howard continued to hold what became known as the Cantor Wives Dinner for the next seven years. One might fairly assume I never showed my face at another gathering, but, to my surprise, I attended all but one. Each one got easier as time started to perform its magic on our wounds. I even started to look forward to catching up with the other wives, sharing pictures of our growing children, and toasting new relationships, second marriages, and even babies. Allison was right; maybe an annual dinner gave us all a precious moment to pause, remember, and raise a glass. At the very least, I learned that a group hug wouldn't kill me.

4

Michael's fifth birthday was October 17, a little over a month after the attacks. I needed my boy to have a traditional birthday party. He should have his friends around him, clapping, while he blew out the candles. I wanted the silliness and racket of a normal celebration.

But I couldn't plan it. Logistics, for some reason, paralyzed me. So did the thought of marking our son's birthday without Doug. Three colorful packages of "Let's Party" invitations sat unopened on my desk. Pam Weinberg once again saved me and stepped in to handle all of the details. She reserved the children's play space at the Reebok Club and asked Michael's karate instructor to hold a demonstration class for the children.

The day before the party, my sister-in-law, Danielle, took Michael for a bike ride in Central Park. Doug's parents came over, as they did nearly every day, and joined my parents and me as we resumed our usual positions in the living room to wait for the day to end. The phone rang, I picked it up, and Danielle's distressed voice rang in my ear: "Jennifer, you have to come here right now. Michael fell off his bike."

"Where are you?" I asked.

"We were just riding slowly up the hill, and he tipped over and hurt his face."

"Where are you?"

"Across from Tavern on the Green."

"Don't move."

I turned to my father, told him to put on his shoes and come with me. My mother and Joe started to get up, but I asked them to stay with Julia until I knew what had happened. I ran through the service door in the kitchen, flew down the stairs, and headed for the park. I remember my father yelling at me to be careful as I recklessly dodged cars on Central Park West, crossing against the light to Tavern's parking lot on Sixty-Seventh Street. I tore past the Bloomberg playground, where Doug and I used to spend hours pushing the kids on swings "so high in the sky." Ahead of me was the entrance to Sheep Meadow, a large grassy field usually overrun with families, hacky-sack players, and sunbathers on a lunch break. I turned right and headed down the drive toward Tavern's outdoor café. There they were. A small crowd had gathered under a tree, surrounding a tiny form—my boy—holding a white towel against his mouth. Danielle paced anxiously on the sidewalk, looking for me.

I reached the tree, bodies parted, and I saw two frightened brown eyes looking up at me. "Mommy," Michael snuffled beneath the towel over his mouth and nose. He started to cry.

"Let me see, honey. It's okay."

Michael let me remove the reddening towel. His face didn't have a scratch on it, but his mouth looked like bloody ground meat. Two front teeth were broken and twisted at bizarre angles.

His lip was engorged with an impressive cut. Blood pooled over his gums and dripped onto the towel. He looked and sounded like a mini Rocky Balboa minus the swollen eyes. I gently put the towel back to his mouth and smiled. "Michael, we can fix this, baby. You're fine. Mommy can fix this." My father sat on the grass with Michael, and I turned to Doug's sister, who was fidgeting with worry and fear. "Danielle, it's okay. Michael's fine. Kids fall off their bikes all the time. We can fix this."

One might think I'd be traumatized to find my son lying injured on the pavement a month after what we had been through. On the contrary, I was elated. His injury energized me in a way that I hadn't felt in a long time. For the first time since the attacks, I could be my child's mother, kiss the boo-boo, and make it "all better." This is what mommies did, and what I could not do for my children when their daddy died. Moms were supposed to fix things, put them back the way they were. But Doug's death couldn't be mended with a few Band-Aids and Neosporin. Standing in Central Park looking at my bloody child, I felt my competence return: *This* I can repair.

The ambulance arrived within minutes, and we bundled Michael onto a gurney. Danielle and I rode with him to the hospital while my father took Michael's bicycle and helmet back to the apartment. My child looked so tiny strapped onto the stretcher. He started to wail. I held his hand tightly. "Michael, you lost a couple of teeth, but they're baby teeth. They will grow back as big-boy teeth. You're fine, Mommy's right here." He continued to sniffle. "Have I told you about the tooth fairy? He brings you a special reward every time you lose a tooth." This got his full attention. For the remainder of the ride, the two EMTs distracted Michael and turned on the siren, bringing a crooked smile to his swollen face.

Roosevelt Hospital's doors are set between two long walls of windows facing the street. When I got out of the ambulance, I almost fell over when I saw that the windows were plastered with hundreds of photographs and flyers of the missing. Until today I had only ventured out to familiar places within a small radius of my apartment. I avoided the news and had never seen an actual "missing" poster. I was not prepared. Snapshots of husbands and wives on their wedding day, smiling recent college graduates wearing fraternity sweatshirts, dads holding infants— a pastiche of ghosts and ruined lives stared straight at me. My breath caught, but I had to keep moving. Worried grandparents poured out of a taxi behind me, and my son still bled through the towel in front of me. We opened the door and walked past the beaming faces on the posters.

The nurse put Michael on the examining table in a sterile, curtained-off area. We told the intake nurse and, frankly, everyone within earshot that Michael's father had died on 9/11. (Wasn't it relevant? It always seemed necessary to mention.) As the doctor began his examination of Michael's wounds, the sturdy blond nurse rubbed my arm and whispered how sorry she was for my loss. I shrank away reflexively. Sometimes a kind word from a stranger unraveled me faster than a tearful embrace from a close friend. Perhaps it was the pure sincerity of the gesture, the kindness that affected me. Or maybe it was that another person had unmasked me again: *So you're not moving through this world like the rest of us.* I was irrevocably damaged and still unsteady. "Would you like a Xanax?" she offered. "It might help you get through this."

I laughed and pointed to my bag. "I have my own. Want one?"

Prior to 9/11, I was afraid of pills and never took anything stronger than Advil. Now, I was the newest denizen of the Valley of the Dolls. Xanax, Valium, Ambien, Prozac—all were at my disposal. Initially, I'd fought with my therapist every time she prescribed a new pill. When I confided to Vicky that the therapist had convinced me to take half a Xanax to calm panic attacks, she responded drily, "Welcome to Manhattan, Jennifer. Where have you been?" I was such a neophyte that I didn't know the answer when Jayme, my nurse practitioner sister, asked how many milligrams I was taking. I told her I'd tossed the prescription bottle and kept the white pills loose in the zippered change section of my wallet in case I needed to swallow one on the sly. Jayme was not amused.

The doctor told me that Michael would need surgery immediately because the impact pushed four of his front teeth deep into his upper gums. The surgeon would pull the teeth back into place and remove the two front ones that had splintered. He told me he'd give Michael twilight sedation: Michael would be conscious but numb. I listened calmly and tried to ask reasonable questions, but I'm not sure I really heard the answers. Michael didn't take his eyes off me. I squeezed his foot, tickled his belly, and assured him that this was nothing he couldn't handle.

Michael woke up with an enormous lip and stitches across his upper gums. Within minutes, Howard Lutnick burst into the room holding a bouquet of balloons that he'd commandeered from the birthday party he'd left upon receiving my anxious call from the hospital. Howard sprawled on the bed, enveloping Michael in his arms. "Michael James. How are you, handsome man? Look at all this attention!"

Later that night at home, I gingerly dressed Michael in his pajamas and put him in my king-size bed with his blue blanket and Daddy's Bear, a plush bear in a white sweater with the Union Jack flag that Doug gave Michael after one of his many business trips to London. Michael looked miniature again, as he had on the gurney, propped up on pillows under the thick duvet. Howard's balloons floated overhead, tethered to the reading lamp. We were watching cartoons when I heard my mother open the front door. In an instant, Howard and his sons appeared at the foot of the bed. Five-year-old Kyle and four-year-old Brandon were also in their pajamas, holding overstuffed cellophane bags of treats from Dylan's Candy Bar. Howard pointed at me and proclaimed in a dramatic voice, "Jennifer, you must leave us now. The men are here for Michael." He and the boys jumped onto the bed and lay on either side of my tiny, swollen boy. I left the room as they all snuggled close.

5

My therapist said my children's young age would protect them. They wouldn't remember the trauma. They had a resilience we adults don't. They bounced back, moved forward, stayed positive. But seeing Michael try to cope without Daddy didn't give me great confidence in my shrink's professional opinion. Michael couldn't sleep. I often woke in the middle of the night to find his wet little face pressed against mine, his tattered blue security blanket wrapped around his hands. "Mommy, I'm thinking about the bad things again," he'd inform me, climbing into my arms. The Bad Things. What else did we ever think about? At least I had Ambien in a pinch; poor Michael was left unarmed to face his nightmares. On particularly anguished nights, I'd carry him back to his room, wrap him in his covers, and rub his back until he fell asleep again. Michael was so little, just a tiny boy in striped pajamas, who should've only had images of baseball fields and *Blue's Clues* in his brain, not fiery buildings and crashing airplanes. The terrorists took not just his father, but his equanimity.

I was extremely reluctant to see a therapist during the first few weeks following the attacks. What brilliant insights didn't I already know? That I was depressed? Anxiety-ridden? That, but for my children, I wanted to throw myself in front of the No. 6 train? Eureka. I didn't need to pay $200 an hour for someone to confirm that my dream life with the man I adored was over. But Michael's nightmares changed my mind about getting help. My children were depending upon me to guide them through the maelstrom, and I didn't have the vocabulary or the game plan. I was nearly catatonic much of the time, struggling with "traffic control" in our overrun apartment. With my parents living with us and the perpetual influx of visitors, I felt as if I had to be "on" all the time—a veritable Stepford Widow—greeting guests with a prim smile and an array of cold drinks. How was I ever going to find our way back to normal with our family in upheaval and the city nearly paralyzed? Maybe a therapist could help me manage at least the logistics of grieving, if not the grief.

It may sound like denial or denseness, but I didn't honestly know how profoundly my son was suffering until he met with Lynn, the blunt-talking, soul-bandaging therapist I came to love. On his first visit, Michael drew a picture of our family. The drawing consisted of four figures—Michael, Julia, and I appeared as stick figures at the bottom of a sheet of paper. Next to the boy figure, he drew Doug. I knew it was his father because Michael sketched a man who needed two pages of computer paper taped together to fit it into the scene. The daddy appeared as a giant; his legs took up an entire page. Lynn explained that Doug's death didn't completely register with Michael; Doug was gone, but he still loomed large and present in my son's concept of family. Lynn also showed me another drawing Michael did of only the three of us without Daddy. Our crudely drawn figures floated at the top of the page.

She told me, "For Michael, his family isn't grounded anymore. Nothing feels stable." It was confirmed: we were all unmoored.

One of Michael's drawings haunts me to this day. As I was putting him to bed one mid-autumn night, Michael pulled from his backpack a special drawing he'd made at school. "Mommy, this is what I'm going to build for you one day," he said, proudly handing me the paper. It was a picture of an apartment building. Not surprisingly, Michael drew many pictures of skyscrapers after the attacks, but this one was different. The drawing showed a rectangular tower divided into a checkerboard of floors and apartments. On the roof of the building, Michael drew a red flashing light and a hose. "This is your room," Michael said pointing to a square at the end of the fourth floor. My room had the thickest, most reinforced walls in the structure. Two figures holding fire extinguishers stood at the door. Outside my window he attached a blue police siren to the wall. Michael had designed a fortress to keep me safe. "This is going to be my apartment," he boasted. "I'm going to live below you, and here are the stairs that go up to your floor from mine." At the base of the drawing in front of what would be the building's entrance, Michael drew two doormen and a fire hydrant.

Every thought behind his childish sketch echoed in my relationship with my son—both after the attacks and even before. In his earliest years, Michael never detached easily from Doug and me. We called him the Barnacle. During the first few days of pre-school, parents participated in separation exercises to encourage their children to interact with each other in the classroom. Parents were asked to remain in the room for a few minutes and then retreat to the "coffee room" down the hall while the children adjusted to their new independence. I never saw the coffee room. For two straight years, Doug or I was the last parent to leave, usually with a final, reluctant wave to a weeping boy struggling to bolt. After the attacks, Michael needed to know at all times where I was. Schedule changes unnerved him; fire drills were the worst. He'd break down unless a teacher called me to convey any change in plans. For a while, if I was not literally standing in the classroom doorway at the moment of dismissal, Michael would be inconsolable. To this day, he still needs to know where I am and worries if I don't answer my cell phone after the first few rings.

Michael wasn't the only one plagued by disturbing dreams. At first, my nightmares were disjointed scenes of me frantically searching for Doug through rubble-strewn streets filled with smoke and gang fighting. Early on, I remember a dream in which I saw myself enter a dilapidated mansion where a fire was blazing in an enormous hearth at the bottom of a once-grand staircase. On the stairs sat a sneering, turbaned man. Trapped in the fire was a white rabbit, screaming while its fur curled into flames. The evil-Gandhi character laughed while I tried to grab the poor dying creature from its pyre. I didn't need a Ph.D. in psychotherapy to diagnose that one.

Most of my visions, however, reflected futile attempts to let go of Doug. Like Michael at preschool, I fought all efforts to separate. I had dreams in which Doug intentionally avoided me. His phone number was wrong when I called it, or he gave me the incorrect address so I couldn't find him. I guess it was his way of teaching me he was gone, pushing me away without a word. Eventually, my subconscious delivered images that were much less subtle. I'd catch glimpses of Doug looking sickly and frail, sometimes holding his head as if he'd suffered an acute migraine or brain injury. The unsettling dream that sent me running to the shrink, however, occurred over a month after the attacks. In it, I'd finally located Doug downtown in a warehouse that resembled the layout of Jeffrey, the retail store. The long, white space had a back room separated from the front by a swinging restaurant door with a round window. I crept to the window and peered inside, where I saw a gathering of men dressed in white attending what looked like a private meeting. Doug was there, also dressed in white, sitting with the other men on wooden crates. I wanted to burst through the door, but I knew I wasn't allowed to enter. Eventually the men filed out silently, each with an empty expression. Doug appeared in the doorway—he looked skinny, gaunt, disheveled. I squeezed his arm and pulled him into a hard embrace. "I thought you'd be mad," he said, his arms hanging limply by his side. "Never. I love you. Come home," I cried into his chest. Then I woke up sobbing.

"I saw him," I nearly shouted at Lynn at our next appointment. "He's still with me. He didn't push me away this time. Maybe he isn't completely gone." Lynn put the kibosh on my reverie. The dream, she told me, indicated exactly the opposite. I wasn't holding on to him, but finally letting go. It was a transitional dream, she explained. Doug appeared to me more dead than alive. He was in my past; I was starting to accept he would never come home.

I told Lynn I wanted a refund for that session.

Doug's absence affected Julia, but it was less obvious to her because she was only two years old. A bubbly and outgoing toddler, Julia was the comic relief in our family—the little pistol who pulled our attention with her mischievous singing and dancing. We called her the Monkey because there wasn't a counter, bookcase, or bureau that she didn't try to climb. I think the overwhelming sadness in the house confused her. Strangers moved in and out all the time, but no one was smiling or dancing with her.

I played with Julia as often as I could. We read stories together and held tea parties with her dolls, but I didn't have the stamina for much more. Candy Land took it out of me. My mind couldn't disengage long enough to allow me to focus for too long. I feel guilty to this day for not giving Julia the focused attention she deserved during such a precarious time.

Julia was too young to say she missed Daddy, but I knew she was missing something. She often chirped, "Daddy died, Daddy died," while running down the hallway. Michael would snap at her to stop, and Julia would be left wounded and confused. I watched her effusive personality become more subdued and stubborn. She'd refuse to eat or throw a tantrum over my grabbing the wrong towel for her bath. Like me, if Julia couldn't control the big things happening around her, she would hold fast to the little things.

My daughter's unknowing campaign to shield herself from the emotional intensity of our home reached a heartbreaking climax one terrible night months after the attacks. My parents, who'd been living with us for four months, finally moved back to Longmeadow to allow me to try to cope on my own. Julia had been diagnosed with strep throat that afternoon, and I was standing with her in the kids' tiny bathroom trying to coax her to take a dose of antibiotics. She adamantly refused the white, viscous liquid. When I held the spoon to her mouth, she pressed her lips together tightly and whipped her head from side to side. "Please, Julia, you have to take this," I begged. "No!" came her screeching reply. "Don't like it!" Within minutes, the gooey medicine was dripping all over her face and pajamas as we struggled. What should have been a three-second transaction turned into a heated battle, ending up with my literally wrestling my intractable toddler to the floor. I was in a panic; I'd read that children could die from strep throat if they weren't treated with antibiotics promptly. I admit her wailing didn't move me. I just didn't have the strength to negotiate. I wrapped my legs around Julia's body in a pathetic attempt to immobilize her. Julia was going to swallow that medicine one way or another.

Her screams and gut-wrenching cries brought Michael to the door. He thought I was hurting her (which of course I wasn't), but witnessing his sister trying desperately to escape my full-body hold was too much for him. "Mommy, stop! You're scaring her." Michael trembled as he gripped the doorknob.

"I'm not hurting her, Michael. She's fine. She has to take the medicine," I retorted over my shoulder, as I grappled once again to maneuver the spoon into Julia's angry mouth.

Suddenly, Julia shrieked at the top of her lungs, "I want Daddy!"

Her outburst struck me like an open-hand slap. I snapped angrily, "He's not here anymore. You're stuck with me!" The room fell silent. Michael paled, and I looked down at Julia's red, anguished face and burst into tears. There we were, splayed on the bathroom floor, sweating and exhausted, completely alone. My heart ached. The kids needed a grown-up, not a terrified, screeching harridan devoid of basic parenting skills. I knew I was failing them, helpless to improve their fatherlessness. Immediately, I loosened my grip on Julia and hugged her gently to my chest. "I'm sorry, Monkey. I'm so sorry. I miss him, too." I sobbed into my baby's neck, our tears mingling with the sticky, white liquid that still covered both of us. I reached up to pull her quaking brother into our miserable embrace, and we rocked all together until our breathing returned to normal.

6

We often hear that veterans of trauma are "changed" by their experience. Suddenly, the survivor is a new person with a fresh perspective. She is kinder, more appreciative of the little things; she's learned that love is all that matters. Maybe, but I don't completely buy it. This widow certainly didn't need a lesson in recognizing what was important.

New York can be an overwhelmingly competitive place, where women especially can get mired in keeping-up-with-the-Joneses. Dolce-clad, chef-fed, driver-driven women with their taut "cores" certainly intimidated me when I first arrived in Manhattan with my week's worth of "good" suits and two pairs of Nine West pumps. But I didn't aspire to the moneyed lifestyle. I was a career girl who honestly dreamed of finding the man who would make me want to leave the office early. Doug was that guy. With him, I knew those women had nothing I wanted. I won't deny that we enjoyed luxuries, but those perks were the icing, not the point, not the glue at all. I used to tell Doug I didn't care if we lived in a tent on the East River, and I meant it. He brought out the best in me and, as long he loved me, I was whole.

Okay, even I'm rolling my eyes, because I can understand how pat it sounds to someone who wasn't inside my relationship with Doug. After marrying him, I definitely joined the ranks of the modishly decked out, professionally coiffed. True, I liked the better wardrobe and vacations. Who wouldn't? But we never took our good fortune for granted. I continued to work at Proskauer, the law firm that first brought me to New York, and eventually joined the legal department at the *New York Times* soon after we were married. We drove a Toyota with two juice-stained car seats strapped to the backseat and Raffi discs jammed in the CD player. Our apartment was comfortable by New York standards, but the cheap green carpet covered in toys and the rubber bumpers on the simple furniture never let you forget that busy toddlers resided there. Living the good life was because of the man on the ride with me—none of it was ever about swag. Doug was the only bling that mattered, and I told him that every day.

·····

I don't think tragedy necessarily changes a person. It does, however, thrust one's core personality into sharp focus. That is what Doug's sudden death did. As a lawyer, I relied on my ability to communicate. Talking, finding the right words, were the hallmarks of my profession and also came in handy whenever I wrote a gushy birthday card or regaled Doug with detailed accounts of his children's daily exploits. My husband's violent death showed me how useless language was to encapsulate the impact of his loss. I struggled to put words to my pain, hoping that if I could somehow reduce the catastrophe into an eloquent précis I'd be able to cope. I was an English major, for God's sake, I should be able to do that. But, describe 9/11? Words failed. Utterly. For months, I tried to share with others what I felt—to lock down the experience with florid language, describing in operatic terms what Doug meant to us. It didn't work at all. The only two sentences that ever came close to accurately assessing the situation were "I miss him" and "This sucks."

Since my verbal skills didn't bring comfort, I turned to dark humor to deflect the misery. Like the Hawkeye Pierce character from *M*A*S*H*, who used sarcasm and irony to try to shield himself from the atrocities of the Korean War, I found that similar tactics worked as a filter through which I could view the aftermath of 9/11 without dissolving. I referred to Doug irreverently and made up pithy labels such as "the widow's diet" in a pathetic attempt to exert control over the uncontrollable and defer the pain until the end of the day when an Ambien would finish the job. Of course, the inappropriate-humor ploy was a short-term fix that ultimately failed to keep the horrors at a safe distance. Hawkeye eventually suffered a psychological breakdown, and I endured anxiety attacks anytime I traveled south of Fourteenth Street.

If it hasn't been made clear by now, I think it's fair to say that I was a type A personality. At a young age, I realized that anything I wanted to achieve would have to come from hard work. I didn't have social connections, movie star looks, or a trust fund. My mother taught me, as she taught her fourth graders, that an inquisitive mind and staying organized were the key to everything. If your bedroom was neat, your notebooks in order, and you were punctual, you'd do well and have peace of mind. I assiduously took her advice and became that person who planned vacations more than a year in advance, answered mail the minute it hit the desk, and color-coded my files. Knowing where everything was had a reassuring effect on me, though I pitied Doug, who often got swept into my frequent cleaning frenzies, when all he wanted to do was watch the U.S. Open. Fittingly, by September 11 I'd already finished the back-to-school shopping for the kids, put all of the summer photos in the album, and mailed Michael's completed school applications for the following year. Everything was done; all I had left on my to-do list was . . . grieve.

After Doug died, I instantly tried to organize my way out of the anguish. Having something to do became an obsession, and I looked for tasks to complete. Doug always managed our finances, but now I had to captain that ship. I quickly learned how to use Quicken and studied our investments so that I could make reasonable financial decisions. I finished the estate filings in record time and filled the kids' calendars with play dates, ballet, soccer, and basketball. Every afternoon I attacked the mail, making neat piles of bills, magazines, and what I scathingly referred to as "death" mail. The death mail was a daily barrage of condolence cards, Red Cross letters, change-of-beneficiary forms, and promotional literature from bereavement camps to investment services. I'd obviously entered a new niche demographic, and the piles of brochures clogging my wastebasket attested to my enthusiasm for that marketing strategy. Death mail was one of the worst things about losing a spouse on 9/11—no matter where I turned or tried to hide, something always appeared to remind me that my husband was murdered.

For the first several weeks, I didn't touch Doug's personal things. His loose change remained on the bedside table, and his hangers and drawers were left untouched. Not surprisingly, when I finally decided to clean out Doug's closets, I did it on a sudden impulse in two frenetic hours. Soon after Michael broke his teeth on the bike path in Central Park, I went into one of Doug's closets to retrieve his blue denim shirt. I'd worn it in the latter stages of both of my pregnancies, and I needed to wallow in its roomy folds. The shirts still hangs in my closet, waiting for Michael to grow into it. As soon as I lifted it from its perch, I immediately started to pull out several other favorite shirts for preservation. This started a flurry of activity, an unstoppable chain reaction of crazed yanking and throwing to the carpet the contents of Doug's racks and drawers into "Save" and "Give to Doug's sister" piles. Hearing the sound of shoes thudding to the ground, my father ran into the bedroom to see if I needed any help. "Daddy, pretend I'm not doing what I'm doing and please just help me make piles," I pleaded from the top of the stepladder as I stretched to reach Doug's upper shelves.

For the next two hours, my dad followed me throughout the house as I gutted every closet and drawer used by Doug. It was definitely too soon after his death for me to do this, but I couldn't stop once I began. "Just get it done—cross it off the list," I repeated to myself as the tears poured down my cheeks. My dad found large garbage bags and stuffed them with armfuls of Doug's clothing. This was as close to a burial as I was going to get—a room filled with black Hefty bags containing the sartorial remains of my husband's life as a businessman, golfer, athlete, and father. I found his collection of cacophonous, multicolored Hawaiian shirts. Doug's attitude about vacation wardrobes was the louder the better, and those crazy shirts didn't whisper. I pulled Doug's wedding tuxedo from the back of the closet. "When did we ever think a double-breasted, shawl-collar tuxedo jacket was the epitome of high fashion?" I mumbled as I handed it to my father, along with the white shirt and matching vest he wore on the day we married.

I stored the purple-striped polo shirt he had on the night we were stranded for several hilarious hours on our friend's stalled sailboat in Sag Harbor Bay. I choked when I pulled Doug's ice-blue linen shirt he bought at J.Crew with me last June. He was so excited to find something in his large size that he bought the same shirt in four colors. There they were, hanging together like a sherbet rainbow. I forced myself to toss all but the one in my hand. I needed to keep Doug's favorite ties (several of which I gave to his father, who wore them for years). I hurled them off their neat racks in rapid succession; the colorful silks fluttered to the carpet in two jumbled piles. The tie he wore to the JCC benefit, the one he was wearing when photographed for his Cantor ID card, the one he wore to Jayme and Scott's engagement party. Every tie was a snapshot, a particular summer night, an overcrowded party, a kiss good-bye at the breakfast table. My father carefully rolled each one and put them away.

I tried to keep the clothing Doug wore in photographs with the kids. His faded polo shirts emblazoned with logos from favorite golf courses. His Haverford T-shirts, several of which I still sleep in. Doug was a hoarder; his closet was like an archaeological dig. "Should I keep all of his basketball gear or do you think storing twenty-three pairs of Champion shorts is overkill?" I asked my dad, trying to lighten the mood. My father looked up from the pile and smirked, "I think it's safe to keep one or two as representatives of the master collection." I threw the shorts and two pairs of basketball sneakers to my father and closed the door to the last emptied closet.

·····

I used to be certain we were living a safe existence. We had a doorman, a trusted sitter, and low-risk office jobs. We didn't scuba dive, hang glide, or even ski much. Nothing was perilous. I remember begging Doug not to walk alone through Central Park at night after basketball games. He told me not to worry: "I'm too big; nobody will hurt me." Who would've predicted that a deserted urban park at midnight was safer than Doug's carpeted office on the 105th floor?

Many people left the city after the attacks. If terrorists could take down the Trade Center, it was just a matter of time before they blew up Times Square, right? But, I couldn't leave Manhattan. The only thing Doug ever asked from me was that promise never to make him move to the suburbs. It was an easy promise to keep: I loved New York as much as he did. And I never would have taken the kids more than a taxi ride from Doug's grieving parents. While everyone else was contemplating moves, I renovated. I dug in my heels and clung to our apartment like a drowning sailor to the hull of his overturned craft. I wasn't going anywhere, but I couldn't bear to live with Doug's ghosts hiding behind our home's every familiar turn. Our bedroom felt like a crypt. Within a few months I'd finalized plans to redesign each of our bedrooms. Fresh paint, new carpets and drapes, would complete the transformation, all of which would occur before the first anniversary.

Without the ability to stop bad things from happening, I became consumed with planning our family's schedules to make the future knowable. Literally days after the attacks, I panicked over what I was going to do with the kids during their two-week winter school break in December. Clearly other matters were more pressing, but with my heightened anxiety, I obsessed over resolving every loose end. I worried about traveling. I worried about not traveling. For the prior ten years, Doug, Howard, and Howard's brother, Gary, threw an annual New Year's Eve party. With two out of the three dead, I couldn't imagine staying in Dodge to witness that heartbreaking milestone alone. Luckily,

Howard and Allison had the same thought. We whisked our families to Florida and spent a morose New Year's Eve staring at each other across a table at the hotel.

My therapist told me I was a "doer," a person who coped by completing tasks. I remember once in a panic I stayed up all night methodically looking through every photo album, reading every card and letter, and opening drawers, closets, and cupboards to inventory everything Doug had left behind. I didn't want to be surprised by a forgotten picture or his old glasses or a pair of cuff links. If I touched everything at once, maybe I'd defuse any time bombs that might ambush me later. I thought I was so clever concocting such a brilliant strategy to organize my way to a shorter, less painful recovery. I boasted to my therapist that I'd figured it out and didn't have to see her anymore. She gave me one of her patented wry looks and stated, "If you're so fine, why are you sitting in fetal position picking at your cuticles?" It was true; I was curled up in her armchair like a nervous house cat.

"But, Lynn, I've gotten so much done. I filed the estate paperwork, cleaned Doug's closets, put the kids on a normal schedule—I should be able to have a handle on this already."

"Jennifer, it's been only a few months. You can't draft a marketing plan to cope with loss. I know you hate hearing this, but you have to give it time."

Time heals all wounds. I despise that cliché. I have only a few virtues, and patience isn't one of them. It dawned on me that it didn't matter how accomplished, psychologically sound, or intelligent a person might be, mourning was the great leveler. I was a textbook widow, nothing more. Being average didn't sit well with me.

"Okay, you win," I conceded, exasperated. "But, tell me one thing. Am I at least getting an A in grieving?"

7

We call my dad Zadie, the Yiddish word for "grandfather." The name suits him, and even the doormen would greet him with, "Welcome back, Zadie," whenever my father came to visit. A roll-on-the-floor kind of grandfather, Zadie could entertain a six-year-old for hours by making furniture "talk," performing magic tricks with a quarter, or crooning syrupy folk songs while strumming his ancient acoustic guitar. Michael and Julia lit up when Zadie walked in the door and barely let him put down his suitcase before they would start to hang from his arms like two monkeys swinging from branches.

My mother, whom we call Nana, was the emotional glue of our family. She was a Jewish mother straight out of central casting—kept an immaculate house without a housekeeper, indefatigably hosted overabundant family holidays, preened about her gorgeous grandchildren to the hapless checkout clerk in the supermarket. She was also the source of my go-getter personality. A teacher of at-risk children in impoverished city public schools, she drummed home to me the same lessons she hammered to her students: a secure future comes from hard work. Education is everything. She wanted us to be curious, bold, busy. She organized our lives with an intensity that sometimes bordered on comical. As a child, I once told her that I found salamanders at the creek near our house. Within a day, my mother plunked on my desk a stack of books on amphibians and set up a terrarium teeming with the creatures. Nana couldn't wait to repeat the process with her grandchildren and never arrived at our home without arm-loads of books and a rolling suitcase filled with art projects.

My parents adored Doug, and I suspect my mother may have carried more photos of him in her overstuffed wallet than she did of me. When my father used to meet my old boyfriends, he would casually drape his arm around my shoulders, look my date in the eye, and proclaim, "Mine." A father's word of warning. When I first introduced him to Doug, not only did my dad neglect to offer his territorial "Mine," I think he made an opening offer for my dowry.

Since the attacks, my parents looked like ghosts, weighed down not just by Doug's loss, but by their daughter's agony. The only thing that hurt me more than telling the kids was seeing my parents struggle to suppress their grief to help me with mine. My parents moved into the spare bedroom in the back of my apart-ment for four long months to provide stability and extra hands to care for Michael and Julia.

·····

How do you raise a child without a father? I certainly wasn't the first woman to contemplate that question, but unfortunately there was no instructional manual. Trying to get an anxious toddler to eat her dinner was hard enough with Doug around to cajole her—without him, I was prepared to raise her on Cheerios and Fruit Roll-Ups. I know women valiantly raise children alone every day—most with full-time jobs and under circumstances more dire than mine. I just didn't think I was as resilient. I only had enough clarity to keep the kids on regular schedules; other than that, I hardly had the strength to play one round of Guess Who?—my children's favorite board game. Worse, I was haunted by that looming "male role model" question: who would be the man in their lives?

Four angels stepped in to assume the mantle of substitute father. The first was Zadie, who, in those early months, was a constant, blessed presence. I'd walk into the kitchen to find Michael sitting on Zadie's lap reading the sports pages. My father shared Doug's encyclopedic knowledge of basketball and eagerly mentored his grandson in the fine art of postgame analysis. He taught Michael how to read the box scores and interpret statistics. I think my son learned how to recognize the words *Philadelphia* and *overtime* before he could read *cat*.

The afternoons belonged to Julia. Zadie was Julia's playmate and captive audience. After school, Zadie would take Julia "exploring" in Central Park, clambering over rocks and through wooded paths until they came home exhausted and covered with dirt. He created David, an invisible boy with a squeaky voice who "followed" Julia wherever she went. I barely had the energy for an weak smile, but Zadie made sure his grandchildren giggled every day. He pulled out all of the imaginary games and tricks he used with Jayme and me as children to give Michael and Julia a semblance of a normal family life, whatever "normal" meant at that point.

Doug's father, Joe Gardner, was the second angel. Tall and

athletic with thinning gray hair, Joe was a classic New York gentleman, who built his real estate business over nearly four decades, one conservative investment at a time. Joe didn't like to take taxis; he drove his old, rattling Cadillac all over the city and would circle blocks tirelessly looking for an open parking space. His pockets always jingled with quarters for the meters. Joe had a formal demeanor and a powerful, occasionally intimidating personality. To Doug's friends, he was always "Mr. Gardner," even though they called other friends' parents by their first names.

Joe's reserved persona cracked wide open when Michael and Julia were born. Underneath all his formality beat the heart of a delighted grandfather, who indulged his grandchildren's every whim. As one could imagine, the sudden loss of their only son crushed Joe and Charlotte. They were ten years older than my parents, but Doug's death instantly aged them noticeably. Joe and Doug were partners and genuine best friends who actively sought each other's counsel on nearly every personal or business decision. For a man who rarely displayed his emotions, Joe labored futilely to conceal his pain after losing his son. It broke my heart to see him reduced to tears in the middle of a sentence, helpless to stop the flow.

Losing a spouse is catastrophic, but losing a child is unthinkable. However, instead of shutting off from the world, Joe and Charlotte pasted smiles on their faces and stayed energetic and affectionate with Michael and Julia. For a long time, Joe stopped by the apartment nearly every day after work just to see the kids even for five minutes. We looked forward to the nightly phone calls from Grandma and Grandpa and weekend lunches at the local diner. Joe attended every basketball game, dance recital, and school play. He even woke up early on Sunday mornings to drive us to Michael's basketball practices in Washington

Heights. I tried to talk him out of this thankless task, but Joe wouldn't budge. He insisted that he loved to sit on the cold gym benches for the "privilege" of watching his grandson run drills with the other boys. Five months after the attacks, Joe volunteered to give Michael's preschool class a guided tour of one of his construction sites, complete with child-size hard hats for each student.

Many families who lost someone in the attacks splintered—tense internecine conflicts erupted into nasty wars between surviving spouses and in-laws over child-rearing and estate matters. We were lucky. As other families were pulling apart, ours solidified. Joe treated me like a daughter and a partner, and it's no exaggeration to say he became like a second father to me.

. . . . .

It may not be surprising that the two grandfathers became heroes when our lives imploded. What *was* unexpected, however, was the remarkable commitment made to the kids by my brother-in law, Scott Feldman, and Doug's business partner and best friend, Howard Lutnick. I don't think either Julia or Michael would be as resilient and buoyant as they are today if it weren't for those two.

Scott and Jayme were in the throes of planning their March wedding when Doug died. They immediately postponed it until after the first anniversary of the attacks to give all of us the year to grieve. Younger than Doug by twelve years (and shorter by nearly a foot), Scott is a robust, clever man whose boyish face made him look more like a teenager than the twenty-seven-year-old fledgling private-equity manager he was. His quick wit and outsize personality commanded a room, and Doug found Scott to be a valuable asset and supportive ally. The two of them could be found slouching on the couch dissecting Tiger Woods's back-swing or commiserating over yet another family weekend with the in-laws. Like my father and Doug, Scott also possessed the basketball gene, but took his obsession one step further. Not satisfied simply to play in a league or watch contests on television, Scott also played the Xbox and Nintendo versions of the game. He insisted that Michael's pop culture education would not be complete without a mastery of *Streetball* and *NBA Live*. There may have been a twenty-three-year age difference between Scott and Michael, but one would never know listening to the two of them banter like fraternity brothers while sprawled on the floor hammering away at their twin game consoles.

After the attacks, Scott and Jayme spent nearly every free moment at our apartment. I needed my sister. She understood what I needed even when I didn't. And Scott took a crash course in multitasking. Suddenly, he had to juggle his devastated almost in-laws and a fiancée who was balancing her own shock with the consuming demands of a nascent career and a helpless sister. No one would have blamed him if he'd simply buried himself in his job and kept his head down until all of us regained our footing. But Scott adored Michael and Julia, and with a light touch he gave himself completely over to them and made sure they knew Uncle Scott would never leave them.

Every Tuesday night, Scott arrived at the apartment after work to see the kids. If Julia was still awake, he would read her a few stories or allow her to adorn him with many of the princess accessories in her costume box. After putting Julia to bed, Scott and Michael would disappear into Michael's room for four quarters of competitive bedroom basketball. Scott often brought a video camera, which he set on a shelf to record their contests. Each "quarter" Scott would stop the action to interview Michael on camera for his play-by-play analysis. Occasionally, if Julia was still awake, she'd provide the halftime entertainment with dance moves, shaking her pink blankie and stuffed animals like pompoms. Scott's dedication to his future niece and nephew floored me. He was young, overworked, and certainly didn't sign up for this. But without a moment's pause, he proved to my children that one doesn't have to be blood to be family.

·····

A few days after Michael's bicycle accident, Howard asked to visit me at the apartment to discuss something that was "bothering" him. At that time, Howard was inundated by one crisis after another. He and the surviving Cantor employees worked nearly twenty-hour days from makeshift office space they'd found in a midtown building. The pressure to rebuild the company amid the chaos of a volatile market and panicked family members was crushing. Funerals, wakes, and memorial services crowded the calendar. The Cantor Relief Fund continued to be run out of the Lutnicks' home, the phones ringing day and night with calls from distraught family members looking to connect with a sympathetic voice. Howard should have been bowed by the strain, but to others Howard always appeared energized and focused. He was tireless, but I knew my friend was running on little sleep and the conviction that he simply had to hold things together.

"I can only stay for a few minutes, but I want to talk to you about your children," Howard said as we settled on the sofa in my family room.

"What's on your mind?" I asked, my curiosity piqued.

"I'm a godfather to Michael and Julia, right? I know *godfather* is just an honorary title, but I've been thinking lately that it has to mean something. Doug was my best friend. One question has been nagging at me ever since Michael got hurt on his bike: What would Doug have done if the situation were reversed? What if I had died? Do I have any doubt that Doug would have taken care of Allison and made sure that she and my kids were protected and loved for the rest of their lives? Of course not."

I was confused. "Howard, you *are* taking care of us. You flew into the hospital like the cavalry minutes after I called you. I speak to you or Allison every day. Michael and Julia love you. I know Doug would be very proud of what you've done for his family."

"It's not enough," Howard said brusquely. "I feel like I made a bigger promise to my friend when I became his children's god-father. I don't want to be merely 'Uncle Howard' to them, the person who sees them once in a while on special occasions and holidays. What kind of commitment is that? It affected me see-ing Kyle, Brandon, and Michael together the other night after Michael came home from the hospital. When we were alone in your room, I made a pact with the boys that we were, from then on, the same family, and Michael would be an honorary brother of Kyle and Brandon. But what does that mean if we're not a real presence in his life?"

"What do you want to do?" I still didn't understand what Howard felt was missing.

"I want to be an *ordinary* presence for your children, not an extraordinary one. I want them to be able to count on me, to know that their dad's best friend is their best friend, too. It's exactly what Doug would do for me." Howard paused and adjusted his glasses as if they'd suddenly become too tight. "If it's okay with you, I'd like to arrange that once a week I'll leave work early to pick up Michael and my boys and take them out for a few hours of 'man time.' I'll come in to see Julia, too, but I want Michael to spend real time with my boys and me. I can tell him stories about his dad and help him understand what kind of man Doug was. It will be good for Michael, don't you agree?"

"I think it will be good for you, too," I said with tears starting to trickle down my face. "I think you boys need each other."

So Men's Night Out was born. Every Thursday, for two straight years, Howard left work by six o'clock regardless of what was happening at the office. He'd ring our doorbell, sweep up in his arms a bathed and pajama-clad Michael, and whisk him away with his own boys to an arcade, Dylan's Candy Bar, or Chelsea Piers for a few hours of playtime and sugary treats. Allison agreed that Howard needed Men's Night Out as much as the boys did; it was the one night each week when Howard could just be Dad and deal with issues no bigger than what flavor ice cream to choose.

Michael always waited by the door for Howard to arrive. Watching Michael leap at Howard made me smile, but it also killed me. These men were the most incredible substitutes, and, of course, no substitute at all. They saved us, and at the same time they confirmed I was drowning. Every time I watched the elevator close at the end of an evening, I felt guilty that this was the best I'd ever be able to do for the kids. They'd never have a real father, as I was never going to love anyone again. I'd become a shell, devoid of feelings other than a mother's natural instinct to protect her children. I would do my part for them, but I was done otherwise.

8

"You know, Jennifer, God only gives you what you can handle." A mother at Stephen Wise offered me this helpful tidbit of philosophy one morning when I arrived at school after a fitful, no-Ambien night. She'd put her hand on my arm and tilted her head to mine when she shared her revelation. I was itching to snap back, "So it's my fault Doug died? Are you saying if I'd only been a slightly weaker person God wouldn't have killed him?" But, I merely thanked her for her kind words. Most people meant well, and it wasn't my job to teach death etiquette. Plus, I didn't want to alienate the parents of my children's friends or make them feel self-conscious around me. The woman was sincere, and I appreciated every small act of kindness I could get, no matter how awkwardly offered.

That doesn't mean, however, that I subscribed to the idea that God, in His infinite wisdom, played a decisive role in the murder of three thousand people. My friends asked whether I blamed God for Doug's death. I didn't. If I believed in God's existence at all,

I also believed He gave us free will. The radical Islamist terrorists who slammed those planes into the Trade Center exercised free will, though they disingenuously justified their actions as manifestations of "God's will." Still, I wasn't ready to let God off the hook entirely. I didn't have the answers, and until I did, I didn't have the energy to pursue my relationship with the Almighty. Like most mothers when confronted with an unruly child, I put God on a time-out. I thought it best for each of us to retreat to neutral corners and cool off before attempting to negotiate a détente.

It wasn't easy to maintain a separate peace with God. I could set my watch to the moment every survivor paraded on the news would utter, "God must have had a plan for me that day." Or worse, "Everything happens for a reason." Tell me, who benefited from Doug's death? How did Doug not make the cut? No matter where I turned, someone was trying to convince me that the Lord would get us through the crisis. One day I listened to a message on my voice mail from a bizarre stranger who'd somehow collected phone numbers of family members. She was a member of a religious order of which I'd never heard and read scripture for several minutes into my voice mail. Acquaintances from different parts of the country sent me books and links to websites filled with meditations and tranquil contemplations, as if I had the attention span to read *Archie* comics let alone religious dogma. Let the record reflect that, when someone is in the immediate aftermath of a sudden loss, spiritual propaganda and how-to-grieve manuals offer faint comfort. The only thing that helps at all is a patient listener or a horse tranquilizer.

Turning away from religion wasn't easy. I've always strongly identified with Judaism and its teachings. I support Jewish causes and have studied my heritage and Jewish history over the years. Doug and I relished creating a Jewish home for our family. His religious education was less extensive than mine, but he was determined to master the customs along with his children. When Michael first started attending our synagogue's preschool, Doug bought *The Complete Idiot's Guide to Understanding Judaism* to help him understand what his son was learning. He kept the book in a drawer next to the bed, sending me into a paroxysm of giggles whenever he threw a new Yiddish phrase or Jewish fun fact at me. We began to light candles on Friday night and created traditional holiday celebrations with both sides of our family. Judaism gave us another way to connect, and I remember Doug once folding me into his arms after a family Shabbat dinner and saying, "You've brought ritual to our life—real traditions that our kids will remember forever. This is what makes a family. It's all I've ever wanted."

His words torment me every time the summer turns to early autumn and the Jewish High Holidays loom. Rosh Hashanah, the Jewish New Year, and Yom Kippur, the Day of Atonement, usually fall in September or early October. They are the most holy of Jewish holidays, during which time Jews ask God to forgive their past sins and inscribe them in the Book of Life for another year. For Doug and me, the High Holidays gave us a moment to pause and contemplate how thankful we were for our happy marriage and healthy children. Every year we'd join Howard and Allison in synagogue to worship as an extended family. Doug and I would sit in the sanctuary with our prayer books open and steal glances at each other. He'd kiss my forehead as we stood while the cantor sang the ancient words of Kol Nidre, Yom Kippur's opening prayer that calls the congregants to gather before God's tribunal. My eyes always welled during the service because I was so grateful for the man who was holding my hand, and the family we were building. Doug and I never asked God for anything at these moments; we just whispered, "Thank you."

Doug was killed a week before Rosh Hashanah, forever casting an immutable pall over the High Holidays. It is why I seethe every time someone says, "Everything happens for a reason." What cause would God have to rip Doug away from his children in such a heinous manner? How could my ethical, philanthropic, deeply empathetic husband not be inscribed in the Book of Life? I'd understand if God had issues with me, but Doug? Impossible. His death was unacceptable, and the High Holiday services became unbearable. To this day I'm still uneasy sitting in a pew without him. I miss him nudging me for the page number or the sound of his knees crackling when he stood for the opening of the ark. Every service feels like a funeral. The minute the rabbi leads the congregation in the recitation of kaddish, the memorial prayer, I fall apart. I chanted that nugget one too many times for too many people.

Ultimately, I don't think God is the cause of what happens to us. If God is anywhere, I'd like to believe He's in the healing and how we respond to that which is beyond our control. There's an old joke about a deeply pious man who is trapped in his house by a flood. As the water reaches his door, his neighbor yells, "Hey, Saul, take this rope, and I'll save you." Saul replies, "No thanks, God will provide for me." The water reaches the second floor, and Saul's neighbor paddles by in a boat making the same offer to rescue him, to which Saul again declines because he believes God will protect him. The scenario repeats itself for the third time, but Saul, now on his roof, declines his neighbor's proposed rescue by helicopter. Eventually, Saul drowns and arrives in heaven to meet God.

Saul: "God, I just don't understand. I've always been a faithful servant to you. I've been charitable, humble, and observant of your laws. How could you abandon me in my time of need?"

God (in a voice not unlike Mel Brooks's): "Saul, I sent you a rope, a boat, a helicopter. What more did you want from me?"

I think that may be the best lesson we can learn from 9/11 or any traumatic loss. We may be helpless to stop bad things from happening, but perhaps God leaves us signs and road maps to help us recover and reconnect, provided we know where to look. My friends, family, and generous members of our Upper West Side community were the ropes, boats, and helicopters who kept us from drowning. Michael's and Julia's needs for a competent parent gave me the impetus to grab hold of the lifelines. Despite my struggle with faith, I continued to raise my children in the Jewish tradition. Watching them attend Hebrew school and teaching them the basic tenets of our faith forced me to find a way to reestablish a connection with Judaism. My son recently celebrated his bar mitzvah, and I was surprised at how joyous it was to see him read from the Torah and uphold his heritage. I rehearsed the prayers with him, sang the hymns from the front row, and recited kaddish in a clear voice. For the first time in years, I felt embraced by a synagogue service, even though Doug was no longer holding my hand. We're now preparing for Julia's bat mitzvah, and I can't wait to hear my daughter chant her trope. God and I might still be working through our time-out, but at least we've found a more comfortable space in which to coexist.

9

_____

"I need to see you in four seasons first."

It was February 1994, and Doug and I'd been dating for nearly six months. We'd just returned to my apartment after a long weekend of skiing in Sugarbush, Vermont, with friends. I've been a skier since I was two years old and spent many family vacations crisscrossing Vermont's mountains. Doug, however, was a warm-weather kid; skiing was something he did reluctantly. One of my favorite memories of that Sugarbush trip was overhearing Doug grumble to himself while trying to schuss down a trail, the running commentary punctuated by curses and amusing rants about why the hell he was doing this when he didn't really have to. That particular evening, as Doug was trying to force the ski equipment into my inadequate, overstuffed closet, he declared that our next trip would be to a beach where the only gear he needed was a pair of sunglasses.

All I heard was _next trip_. For a single twenty-seven-year-old girl who was falling madly in love with a boyfriend who brought words such as *gallant* and *noble* to mind, the words *next trip* rang like church bells (or in my case, perhaps a shofar). I knew I wanted to marry him, but we'd been together too short a time to confess that. Maybe Doug wasn't thinking about marriage. What guy contemplates marriage without a subtle nudge from his girl-friend? I probably should've just left things alone, but a girl needs to know, right? Before I could stop myself, I coyly asked whether he'd ever thought about marrying me. Without taking a beat he replied, "I need to see you in four seasons first."

"What do you mean, four seasons?" I asked incredulously, but I knew from his tone that Doug was just as smitten as I.

Doug chuckled and crossed his arms, "Well, it took you a hun-dred days before you felt strongly enough about us to introduce me to your law school friends. Now you're going to have to wait. I think I should see you in four seasons before I decide whether or not to keep you. We've come through fall and most of winter just fine. Spring and summer are around the corner."

I feigned exasperation. "But, honey, you said you're the best thing that ever happened to me. I accept your wisdom."

Doug closed the closet doors and turned to me. "And you're the best thing that ever happened to me. I love you. Let's eat."

"Fine," I said with a wry smile. "But, by the way, June twenty-first is first day of summer."

·····

On July 12, Doug and I returned from a day of window-shop-ping in Southampton to Allison and Howard's summer rental in Quogue. They'd gotten engaged in April and were busy planning their December wedding at the Plaza hotel. Howard proposed during an intimate dinner at March, an intimate restaurant tucked into a row of town houses across the street from my apartment. Before dinner, Howard gave Doug a ride to my place after work and called me to join them in the car to see the ring before Allison arrived. I jumped in the backseat of the black limousine parked outside my lobby, and Howard handed me a breathtaking yellow diamond set between two smaller white diamonds on a gold band. To my untrained eye, the ring looked as if it should come with two personal bodyguards. I gasped and handed it back to Howard.

"I don't even want to touch it. That ring is crazy."

"Doug, I told you she'd love it," Howard chided as if this were all a ruse to get Doug to accelerate his own ring search.

"You're killing me," Doug replied, rolling his eyes. "We're so happy for you. Have a wonderful night."

"We love you both," I added. "Good luck!"

I was excited for them and, of course, hoped that we would soon follow their example. But on that lazy summer afternoon, there didn't seem to be much chance of that happening. We'd both taken the week off from work and arrived the night before to enjoy a few quiet days before Allison and Howard arrived for the weekend. Doug, who didn't like the sun, stretched out on a couch in the living room and was soon deeply engrossed in *The Alienist*. I flitted around the house looking for something to read by the pool. The coffee table was piled high with old magazines and newspapers, but I'd already read every one of them. Feeling peevish, I started whining to myself, "There's nothing to read." Doug shifted on the couch and continued to read. I kept on harrumphing.

"Honey, did you hear me? There's nothing to read."

"I'm ignoring you."

Clearly, I was not going to let that stand. I dove onto the couch and draped myself on top of him. Doug groaned and lifted the book to read over my head. I started nuzzling his cheek with my nose. "I'm bored."

"I know, but what does that have to do with me?"

"C'mon, honey. Play with me, please?"

Doug closed his book and stared at me with a slightly annoyed but teasing look in his eyes. He shifted me from his chest, stood up, and stomped to the bedroom. "Come here," he growled over his shoulder. I obediently followed and watched Doug move around the bed to the bureau, where he pulled something from the top drawer.

"Here, you pain in the ass, read this." He laughed, tossing a periodical onto the comforter. It was *Bride* magazine. I looked up at Doug's beaming face and started to quake.

"Are you serious?" I asked, the tears forming.

"Honey, of course I am. I was going to do this later tonight, but you just gave me an opening I couldn't resist."

Doug led me to sit on the edge of the bed. In his hand was a small, black velvet box opened to reveal a delicate platinum band with a simple, round diamond. Stroking my cheek, Doug said the words I'd been waiting for: "I love you, Jennifer. Will you spend the rest of your life with me? Will you marry me?" I nearly smothered him in tears and kisses, a staccato of yeses flying out of me rapid-fire.

"Are you happy?" Doug asked after I stopped hyperventilating.

"So happy."

"Do you like your ring?"

"It's beautiful. I love you."

"I love you, too, so much. You are truly the best thing that ever happened to me. Now, go call your mother. I'm going to read."

I still have the ring. It's just as sparkly as it was the day Doug put it on my finger, but now it lies in a bank safe-deposit box. I can't wear it anymore. It's too happy. Someone suggested I use the diamond in a necklace, but I can't bear to change the setting. I'm saving it for Michael to give to his future wife someday.

Jewelry, birthday cards, favorite T-shirts: what relics remain to soothe a wife after her husband dies? I don't even have Doug's wedding ring because he was wearing it that morning. I heard the city collected hundreds of loose wedding bands and watches that can't be claimed because the pieces didn't have identifying inscriptions or were found without a trace of their owner's body. What I do have, however, is a sealed plastic evidence bag filled with sickeningly twisted and filthy credit cards, driver's license, gym pass, and Cantor Fitzgerald ID card. The police recovered the contents of Doug's wallet somewhere amid the wreckage of the Trade Center and presented them to me in an unceremonious exchange at One Police Plaza four months after the attacks. I'd been summoned by a letter stating that the police had found "documents" belonging to my husband. I thought they meant files or papers from his office. I wasn't expecting to receive such a horrifying envelope containing the irrefutable proof that my husband didn't go gently into that good night. On the subway ride home, I looked at the other passengers in the car and wondered if they could tell I was carrying my husband in my purse.

I didn't realize how difficult it would be not to have a cemetery plot. At first, I was strangely relieved that we didn't have to bury him. The mere idea that I would shovel dirt onto his coffin in the traditional Jewish graveside ceremony frightened me. But, without a coffin or a grave, where would I visit him? Eventually I found my answer in the various rooms and objects donated to charitable organizations in Doug's name. He amassed an eclectic collection of memorials, including a ginkgo tree, children's play spaces in two community centers, a pre-school art classroom, a basketball tournament, and a communal room at NYU Business School poignantly donated by Doug's father, with his and Doug's portraits hanging solemnly side by side on the wall.

None of these generous gifts work as a substitute for a tranquil gravesite. The closest we have is a bench in Central Park. Located just north of the West Side entrance to the Sheep Meadow, the bench sits next to a clearing where Doug and I took our annual family photo. On it is a silver plaque bearing Doug's name and the words YOU ARE OUR HERO. WE LOVE YOU FOREVER.

I wish I could say that I found comfort sitting on his bench, that I felt closer to him when I was there. But all I ever felt was emptiness. I tried to imbue the bench with a talisman-like power, but all that came to mind when I was stroking Doug's plaque was Shelley's famous poem "Ozymandias":

> *. . . Two vast and trunkless legs of stone*
> *Stand in the desert. Near them on the sand,*
> *Half sunk, a shattered visage lies . . .*

The lives we build—the monuments we erect for ourselves—all eventually crumble and disappear. Memories turn gray and fade as soon as the next cataclysm lands on the front page of the newspaper. How would I ever keep my beautiful husband's image alive, his memories crystalline?

I knew Doug would be discomfited by all of the memorials. He was modest and preferred to do his philanthropic work "under the radar," as he liked to say. But now that Doug was gone, all I wanted to do was emblazon his name on every lamppost, city bus, billboard, and T-shirt—all in a futile bid to prevent time from diluting the sharp pain of his absence. Unfortunately, none of the rooms, benches, plaques, or events brought any relief. They were the "lifeless things" as Shelley described and, for me, stark reminders that memories and monuments were cold substitutes for Doug's bulk and warmth at the end of a long day.

Then something happened that restored my faith that, perhaps, some tributes are more than a hunk of granite. On one of his Men's Nights Out, Howard came over early to talk to me about a project on which Doug and he had been working. Howard was chairing a fund-raising drive to build a new athletic center at Haverford College and had made a substantial donation to name the facility after his deceased parents, Jane and Solomon Lutnick. Doug was an enthusiastic member of Howard's committee—as everyone knew, no one loved Haverford sports more than my husband. He regaled me frequently with nostalgic stories of his glory days as a tenacious strong forward with his pal, Calvin Gooding, feeding him the ball on demand. Howard sat with me in my kitchen and confessed he was troubled by his decision to name the athletic center after his parents.

"My parents were artists. They didn't care about sports. I don't feel right naming it after them."

"I don't think it matters whether they cared about sports. It's your project. You can name it after anyone you like."

"I know, but it just doesn't feel right.'

"Would you consider naming it after Gary?" I knew Howard still hadn't allowed himself to mourn his brother's death. Maybe naming the facility would give him some relief.

"No, it doesn't feel right to name the center after my brother either. I'll do something else for Gary." Howard leaned toward me. "To be honest, if it's okay with you, I'd really like to name the entire building after Doug."

I couldn't believe what I was hearing. Joe Gardner had already made a gift to name the basketball court after his son, which I thought was the most fitting tribute. And now Howard was offering to honor his best friend with the entire building. It was overwhelming.

"Seriously, Jennifer. I want to call it the Douglas B. Gardner Athletic Center. Don't you think that makes more sense?"

I was stunned. Even my unassuming husband would've been thrilled to have his name synonymous with Haverford athletics. "Howard, are you serious? Is this really what you want to do?"

Howard nodded. "I'm telling you, I've been thinking about this for a while. I want my friend's name on the building. It's the right thing to do."

For the first time since the attacks, I felt Doug again—bodily, as if his arms were around me like a heavy coat draped over my shoulders. I imagined him nodding and smiling at Howard.

"You've made us an offer I can't refuse. It's so perfect. I can't think of anything more Doug than this."

Howard's extraordinary gift to us became an even more significant one for Calvin Gooding's family. Joe and Howard agreed that, in exchange for naming the facility after Doug, Joe's donation would name the basketball court after Calvin. Now both Doug and Cal, the two former teammates, colleagues, and devoted friends, would forever be connected at their beloved alma mater.

At the groundbreaking ceremony months later, Haverford invited me to say a few words before the small crowd gathered around the cordoned area. The proposed facility was to be called the Douglas B. Gardner Integrated Athletic Center. Haverford referred to it in promotional materials as GIAC. Doug's friends and I weren't enamored with the name. It sounded too sterile and impersonal for something bearing Doug's warm moniker. During my short, halting speech I tried to lighten the mood by mentioning that Haverford could identify the center however it wanted, but Doug's friends and I had decided to call it the Doug. The Doug seemed more apt, more in keeping with my husband's jovial, informal personality. When I arrived at the new facility's dedication ceremony two years later, I learned that Haverford's student body had inexplicably adopted the "Doug" as the unofficial name of the facility. If God and I hadn't been on a time-out, I would've thanked Him for sending me a sign that a good name endured, and Doug's name was more than just a word on a wall.

At the end of the program, Howard unveiled the center's engraved plaque, which featured a nearly life-size photograph of Howard and Doug standing side by side smiling with their arms clapped around each other's shoulders. Howard proudly took Michael and Julia by the hands and brought them in for a closer look at the photograph.

"Isn't this a great picture of your dad and me?"

Michael pointed to Howard's image and said, "I know you're standing on a step in that picture. You're not as tall as Daddy."

He was right. How could anyone ever be that tall again?

10

After the Cantor Wives Dinner, I made a concerted effort to will myself back into a less fraught, more even-keeled friendship with Allison. Every time I saw her, I cursed my impulse to dwell on what was missing and focused on how much I wanted to recapture the breezy, giggly, intimate connection we had before 9/11 forever changed the landscape. Allison was patient; she never pushed me to move faster than I could manage, but she also never left me alone to wallow in solitude for too long. A phone call, an invitation to brunch, or a gossipy e-mail would reconnect us. We never discussed our rocky first few months—what was the point? What mattered was the future, and neither of us was going to face it without her best friend in tow. As the frenzied activity in the Lutnick household eventually subsided and I began to adapt as a single parent, we found time to breathe and fell back into a semblance of our familiar routine of late-afternoon manicures and play dates with our children. I even helped her and Edie Lutnick organize Cantor's charitable auction for the Relief Fund held in June at Sotheby's. Famous vendors from around the world generously donated vacations, jewelry, clothing, art, and sports memorabilia to support Cantor's efforts to care for its 658 families. Drafting and inputting descriptions of each auction lot for the journal kept my mind occupied and allowed me to feel useful again. It was energizing to contribute to the team, but it was recovering my bearings with my best friend that really saved me.

By early summer my social life had taken on a predictable pattern. If I needed to get out of the house, I could call Allison and ask, "Take a widow to dinner?" No matter what they were doing, Allison and Howard always made me their "plus one." With the Lutnicks I didn't have to venture into the world as an untethered former wife. Cocooned in their posse, I still felt like a married woman continuing a facsimile of the life I had with Doug. These "pass the widow" arrangements among my close friends (Pam and Vicky were also always reliable participants) were familiar and routine now; it was all the variety I needed outside of raising Michael and Julia.

Not only did I tag along with Allison and Howard in the city, but we took our act to the Hamptons that summer as well. Doug and I had just moved into the summer home we built in the northwest woods of East Hampton the previous year. It amazed me how quickly we put that place together—from dirt to house in nine months. What amazed me more was that Doug chose the Hamptons at all. His childhood summers were spent with his family in Seaview, a village on the narrow strip of land off the coast of Long Island called Fire Island, known for its uncrowded beaches, family-run general stores, and casual lifestyle. No cars are allowed; residents ride rusty bicycles and pull little red wagons to haul groceries or toddlers, and deer roam freely without fear of people. Doug and his sister were second-generation Fire Islanders (their parents met during a beach volleyball game in the fifties) and seemed to know everyone. Doug loved the no-frills, almost bohemian lifestyle there and made his mark every August in the spirited annual basketball tournament.

Doug's parents still lived in the same beach house, a rustic two-story structure with an airy master bedroom and kitchen upstairs, and a warren of children's bedrooms and a cozy sitting area on the first floor. Every weekend we'd pack our car and race to the Bay Shore dock to catch the ferry to Seaview. We'd sip New England clam chowder out of styrofoam cups, hurriedly purchased at the snack kiosk off the parking lot, and huddle together on the ferry's metal benches against the wind coming off the Great South Bay.

Each summer, we aired out Doug's childhood bedroom and moved in; the room ultimately became a nursery when Michael and Julia arrived. As the years went on, many of Doug's Fire Island friends started families and left their childhood board-walks to spend summers in the Hamptons or Westchester. Some were drawn by the social fizz, better restaurants, more to do on a rainy day. Doug was lured by the golf. His burgeoning obsession wasn't slow or subtle. He was infatuated. His unquenchable pas-sion for basketball remained, but Doug started to feel the physi-cal thumping he was taking on the basketball court and noticed the toll on his knees and ankles. He went from playing strong for-ward, fighting for rebounds, to launching three-point shots from nearly half-court, just to protect his rebelling joints. Golf was a welcome respite from the pounding. Fire Island had beaches, boats, and barbecues, but no fairways. The Hamptons had many.

We hadn't spent any time in the Hamptons since the summer we got engaged at the Lutnicks' rental in Quogue. We decided to try renting farther east on the South Fork for July 2000. The tiny ranch house in East Hampton had no lawn and a vinyl pool, but it was close to Pam and Matt Weinberg, and less than a five-minute drive to the nearest golf course. Doug played every day and found a morning pickup basketball game with former Fire Islanders and friends from the city. Two weeks into our rental, he told me to call a real estate broker.

On our first excursion with the broker, we were shown a cleared parcel of land "north of the highway" (the Hamptons' tonier properties lie "south of the highway"). It was located in the crater of an old asphalt quarry, set back from the road and hidden by dense woods. I looked around and thought, "Drainage issues." Doug put his arm around me, pointed to the back of the property, and said, "Basketball court." The next day he made an offer. I was dumbfounded by my husband's impulsiveness. I tried to convince him that we should rent for another summer—what was the rush? Doug wouldn't budge: "This is what I want for us. You get a lawn, I get my court."

We quickly approved construction plans and worked feverishly to get the house ready for Memorial Day weekend 2001. Somehow we finished it on time—a shingled, two-floor, post-modern house with white trim and a circular driveway anchored by a magnificent red beech tree. The house had a wood-burning fireplace, wide wooden porch, and his-and-her sinks in the master bath (a luxury we had never before experienced). The décor was a hodgepodge of inexpensive, slipcovered furniture and hand-me-downs. The place was ready for the holiday weekend, though the yard was still a pit of dirt and construction debris. Doug didn't care about the muddy mess; he was giddy to have his own house. The first morning he ambushed me in the kitchen, shouting excitedly, "Look what I have, honey! Look!" It was a garage-door opener. "I've never had one of these before."

A city boy who lived his whole life in Manhattan apartment buildings with superintendents, Doug never needed to fix a broken appliance or spackle a wall. Suddenly he was evangelical about home repair. The first time he used a power drill to hang hooks in the garage, we captured the moment in a photograph that is still Scotch-taped to the refrigerator.

That first and only summer together in our new house was out of a movie. Doug swam with the kids in the pool, turned hot dogs and steaks on our not-yet-rusted grill, and found his lounging spot on the green-striped couch on the shaded deck. When his exalted basketball court was finally paved, the white lines drawn and regulation glass backboards raised, Doug held an inaugural "run" with his buddies in early August. Of course, he hit the first shot, provoking shouts of "Fix!" and "Home court!" from the other players. Four-year-old Michael watched the game from his perch on the large plastic cooler filled with bottled water and Gatorade; he proudly handed the cold drinks to sweaty players after each eleven-point contest. Julia sat on my shoulders waving at her daddy every time he ran by. The Sunday-morning pickup game had found a new home in our backyard, and my husband was visibly thrilled.

Doug joined a local golf course and scheduled predawn tee times to get back in time for lunch with us. (Okay, he also managed to sneak an additional nine holes at four o'clock on a few afternoons if all seemed quiet on the home front.) On my thirty-fifth birthday in August—our last month together—Doug hosted a small dinner party in our new living room. We cleared the furniture and set up tables with light blue tablecloths and centerpieces of white roses. He opened his toast with "Welcome to our house that Jenny built."

· · · · ·

A year later, I was living alone with Michael and Julia in our barely touched house in the woods, the white lines on the basketball court still looking freshly painted. Doug didn't live to see the gravel spread on the driveway, the spring growth on our newly planted deer-resistant shrubs, or the wooden swing set I had installed in April. On what would have been his fortieth birthday, less than a month after the attacks, the kids and I drove from the city to our house to mark the day. We took two boxes of Doug's favorite Product 19 cereal out of the kitchen pantry and carried them to the duck pond on Davids Lane. Our kids loved to feed the ducks there, and Daddy always had a seemingly endless supply of crumbled bread for them to toss to the mallards and swans that congregated in that tranquil cove. I handed the cereal boxes to Julia and Michael and helped them scatter Daddy's flakes on the water. *Happy birthday, my love.*

That our house gave me comfort surprised me. For the first time since the attacks, I could finally sit still. This place was ours, a safe haven, without any memories except those that Doug and I had made. It wasn't a renovated apartment or an inherited family home, it represented an entirely fresh start, a realization of everything we'd fantasized about together. But at the same time none of it filled the emptiness. Grieving is the great leveler, and no amount of wisdom, fresh paint, or retail therapy insulates anyone from its tenacious grip. I felt Doug everywhere, from his unlaced basketball sneakers still waiting by the sliding glass doors to the showerhead installed six inches higher than normal to accommodate his height. Every press of the garage-door opener or hiss of the barbecue cut into me with jagged strokes. And I constantly replayed what he whispered to me on one of our last evenings there. After the kids went to bed, Doug took me outside to look at the new backyard and, holding me in his arms, promised that this home would be "where we will make our memories."

On clear summer nights after the kids went to bed, I would walk through the sliding glass door from my bedroom to the porch and, in the stillness, talk to my vanished husband. I cried over the hydrangea bushes pushing through the white railing, remembering when we picked them out at the nursery the year before. Still, I thanked Doug out loud for giving us this house and demanding that it be built so quickly. It occurred to me that perhaps some higher power knew we had to get it done, or that Doug intuited he had to make a refuge for his family. How could he have known how important this private sanctuary would be to our recovery? The house that Doug built became our serene escape from a frantic city life, where anxiety nagged below every skyscraper and loss pervaded every conversation.

⋯⋯

At the start of Fourth of July weekend, ten months after the attacks, I was in my usual place at dinner with Allison and Howard. We were at Saracen, a popular Italian restaurant in the Hamptons, along with Allison's brother, Gary, and Karen, a friend of hers from high school. Next to us, we noticed three good-looking men drinking martinis and finishing a round of appetizers.

"Do you think they're gay?" someone posited.

We furtively looked at the other table, and Karen gave a noncommittal shrug, "They could be; not clear." We filled a few minutes analyzing the men's grooming, body language, and neat attire, then returned to our dinner without drawing a conclusion.

The Lutnicks were renting their first Hamptons house since

their marriage. They used to spend every summer in London, where Howard would run Cantor and be closer to the firm's European operation. Doug managed the New York office while Howard was away. After 9/11, everyone stayed home. Howard liked to tell me that he told his broker the most important aspect of any potential rental was that his house could not be "more than ten minutes away from Jennifer's."

At the end of dinner, Karen and I got up to go to the ladies' room. We were walking through the crowded bar on our way back to the table when I caught a glimpse of Billy Joel sitting in the corner, talking to a red-haired woman. I stopped to get a better look. At that moment, a man in front of me stepped backward and squashed my toe under his foot.

"Ow!" I said a little more sharply than I intended.

The man turned around. "I didn't step on your foot, did I? I didn't feel anything."

"I don't think I'm lying," I replied, still looking down at my foot.

"I'm sorry about that. I was trying to look at Billy Joel over there. I'm Derek."

I looked up and realized that he was one of the three men we'd been discussing at dinner. Dressed in a tight black T-shirt and dark blue jeans, he looked as if he had just stepped out of a Ralph Lauren ad—tall, sun-kissed, with the graceful build of a professional swimmer. He had clear blue eyes deeply set in a sculpted face with a sharp jawline and delicate nose. His thick brown hair was slicked back in a modern James Dean style with flecks of gray playing about his temples. Even in my numbed state, I was thrown by Derek's handsomeness. We don't get many specimens like him in the East End.

"I'm Jennifer," I said, shaking his outstretched hand. "This is Karen." I pulled Karen close and positioned myself slightly behind her. Derek was standing with the two other men from his table. He introduced us to his friends, and the conversation quickly turned to our impressions of Billy Joel and his date. Immediately, it became apparent that these men were straight—there was an instant flirtatious energy. Karen, a pretty, dark-haired woman who was single at the time, kept the conversation light and relaxed. Still, I felt uncomfortable talking to new men—in a bar—and excused myself to walk back to our table. But something made me get up again, and soon I rejoined the group at the bar. Derek deftly maneuvered me into a private conversation.

I probably looked like every other thirtysomething woman trying to meet a man, but really, I was in hell nursing a chardonnay amid the din of the Hamptons singles' scene. Still, Derek was friendly, and Karen seemed to be having a good time, so I took a sip of the wine and kept up my end of the banter. I told myself it was good practice to talk to someone outside my protective circle. I tried to adopt a confident, slightly wry tone, which I hoped would ward off any inquiries that might require me to reveal my situation.

"Do you live in the city?" Derek asked.

"Yes."

"Do you live with roommates or have your own place?"

"I own my own apartment."

"Do you rent a beach house here with friends?"

"No, um, I own my house."

"You own an apartment in the city and a house out here? What do you *do* for a living?" How was I going to answer that without telling him my story? I parried the question and steered the conversation to Derek's life story.

"So, Derek. Where are you from?"

I learned that he'd moved to New York six months earlier from Seattle, where he'd lived his entire life. He was a successful commercial real estate broker there, but felt antsy; life as a thirty-five-year-old bachelor in his hometown had become stale and predictable. Derek wanted a "bigger pond" to "jump-start" his life in a new city.

"What I think you're telling me," I quipped, "is that you dated every available girl in the Seattle metropolitan area, and now you need a new hunting ground."

He laughed, but didn't entirely deny the accusation. In fact, he openly discussed the difficult process he went through to leave his family and friends. He took a chance on a new chapter, giving up a comfortable lake house in favor of a tiny three-bedroom apartment with two roommates in a generic West Side building (two blocks from my apartment, coincidentally). It was actually nice to listen to another person's story, unconnected to 9/11. Like a minivacation. "Derek, I'll bet New York women love that you're a 'fish out of water.'" I lamely kept teasing him about women, but it was all I could think of to keep the conversation away from me.

Again, Derek laughed with no denials. "It is a good hook, I agree."

He took a sip of his cocktail, then asked me to hold his glass for a minute. I took his drink in my free hand while he pulled something that looked like a white Sharpie out of his front pocket.

"What is that?" I asked.

"Insulin. I'm a type one diabetic." He adjusted the dosage and stabbed the long, thin needle into his thigh, right through his jeans. Then he slipped the injector into his pocket and took his drink from my hand. The entire process took maybe seven seconds.

"That was amazing! I've never seen anything like that before," I said, trying not to admit being rattled by it. "Does it hurt?"

"It's like brushing my teeth. I was diagnosed when I was twenty-eight, which is rare since most type one diabetes is discovered in young children. I'm lucky because I was an adult when I found out and relatively mature enough to manage my health."

"I imagine you have to watch your diet."

"I do. I need to be careful about what I eat and how I exercise. I ride road bikes and train for triathlons to stay healthy."

I couldn't resist. "That vodka martini in your hand must be an integral part of the program."

He laughed and raised his glass in a mock toast. "Exactly. I'll have you know that this has one of the lowest sugar contents of any cocktail."

As we continued to chat, it struck me that Derek was more substantial than I had imagined. After a while, I felt more comfortable. We could barely hear each other above the gathering swarm at the bar; each time one of us spoke, he or I had to lean in to speak directly in the other's ear. I spent most of the conversation on tiptoe. It may have looked like flirting, but I didn't feel anything. Okay, yes, he was definitely the best-looking man I had ever seen outside GQ magazine, but it honestly didn't matter to me whether the conversation continued or ended on the spot.

I noticed that Howard and Allison had moved to a table closer to the bar and were keeping an eye on me from a distance. Suddenly it occurred to me that this was the wrong snapshot. I was not supposed to be the one gabbing in a man's ear at a bar on a holiday weekend. I was supposed to be with Doug, sitting with the married couples, watching Karen and our other single friends socialize. The façade I was selling to Derek started to slip, and I felt him touch my arm. "Are you okay?"

That was it. That one gentle, innocent question broke the dam. I was bad at pretending. Struggling to control the pitch of my voice, I told him the truth.

"No, I'm not okay. To be honest with you, I'm thirty-five years old, the mother of two children, and I lost my husband in the World Trade Center. This is very new for me, and I don't know what I'm doing. I'm sorry to throw this at you mid-conversation, but I just needed to say it. You have my permission to run for the door."

Derek looked at me for a moment, very still. A look of recognition passed over his face, as if I confirmed something he suspected all along. "I knew something was different about you," he said, nodding, "you're not like anyone I've met here. I had a feeling there was something going on. I could tell you were a grown-up, but I didn't realize this was why."

"It's been an impossible time for me. I moved with the kids out here for the summer. My best friends are always with me, they're sitting over there. You may recognize the husband from the news: he's Howard Lutnick, the chairman of Cantor Fitzgerald, the company that lost the most employees in the attacks. My husband was Howard's best friend."

I thought we would shake hands and say good-bye, but instead Derek started asking about my children. He wanted to know their names, ages, what they liked to do. He asked how they were handling their father's loss and whether they talked about it. I couldn't believe this bachelor was asking me what cartoons Michael and Julia watched. He then said something I will never forget.

"Jennifer, you've been through the most unimaginable tragedy. I wouldn't wish this on anyone. But maybe one day you'll see that your life is still an adventure. You can choose where you should go from here. You have the opportunity to do anything—not that you want to do anything right now—but maybe someday you'll want to make a new start, and you'll have options that you may not have had before. Look at me. I'm in a crazy transition also. I left behind my life in Seattle to start over in Manhattan. Of course, my story is nothing like yours, but in some ways we're in a similar place."

My head was spinning. Similar place? He *chose* to restart his life. I just wanted my old life back.

"May I say something else? You just said you spend all your time with people who were directly affected by 9/11. That must be comforting and safe, but isn't it also overwhelming after a while? Maybe it would be a good change for you to spend some time with people who had nothing to do with that day. Like with me. Don't get me wrong, I'm not hitting on you, I promise. But I'd like to be your friend if I can. I could tell you more stories about Seattle or be your harmless escort to a party, and maybe you could give me an insider's perspective on New York. I'm in transition, you're in transition—maybe we could have coffee when we get back to the city and help each other through this weird time."

I didn't know what to say. Something about Derek's Pacific-Northwestern open sincerity made me believe him. It also made me want to weep. So instead of unraveling, I quickly thanked him for his kind words and said good-bye. I grabbed Karen by the arm and walked directly out the door into the dimly lit parking lot, where I burst into heaving sobs in the darkness. Karen rubbed my back, while Allison and Howard approached from the restaurant. We stood there for a while until I regained my composure.

"This is just too hard for me. I can't do this," I sniffled. Allison hugged me as Howard and Karen tried to convince me I was brave and doing so well. Suddenly, two bright lights appeared and a silver Porsche convertible roared to a stop right in front of us. It was Derek.

"Hey, Jennifer, can I talk to you for a minute?"

Vanity kicked in, and I turned away from the lights to flip my hair and wipe the mascara from my eyes. I calmed my face and walked tentatively over to the idling car.

Derek draped his elbow over the door and leaned toward me with a warm smile. "Listen, I'm a good guy. I'm not a serial killer or anything like that. I meant what I said inside. I really do think you should look at your life as an adventure; it just might be good for you to break out of your routine and take a chance on something completely new. I hope you'll have coffee or a drink with me sometime. Totally innocent, I promise."

"Okay, I'll think about it," I heard myself say. "My name is Jennifer Gardner. Um, do you want my number?"

"Jennifer Gardner who lives on Central Park West. Don't worry. I'll find you."

Derek put the car in gear and pulled out of the driveway, the gravel crunching loudly under the tires. I stood dazed, watching his car join the traffic on Montauk Highway. Howard walked over and put his arm around my shoulder. "Well, if you're going to cry, at least you're crying about a good-looking guy in a Porsche."

11

The remainder of the Fourth of July weekend was a blur of barbecues, play dates with the kids, and spin classes—nonstop activity. The previous year, Doug and I took Michael and Julia to watch the fireworks at Main Beach in East Hampton. We parked far from the ocean and joined the procession of families schlepping blankets, folding chairs, and coolers to watch the show from a prime sandy spot on the beach. Doug carried Julia on his shoulders, as Michael and I tried to avoid the cracks on the sidewalk. The kids loved the light show—the booms and hissing of the explosions, the dazzling colors. It was another picture-perfect family moment from a Lifetime movie—one that I see now was too perfect to be repeated every year, the way I assumed it would be.

Early Monday morning, I drove the kids to their day camp near the airfield in East Hampton. Julia always bounded out of the car into her counselor's waiting arms. Michael was more tentative. He liked camp, especially since his best friend, Benjamin

Weinberg, was there, but told me that he started to think about the "bad things" whenever he had downtime. The lulls spent moving from one activity to another or waiting on the sidelines for his turn at bat became an eternity, leaving him susceptible to intrusive thoughts. It broke my heart to think about my boy sitting poolside on his towel, his fears overwhelming his mind while he tried to listen to a counselor demonstrate the crawl stroke. I knew how he felt: madness in a vacuum. It swept in at the slightest invitation. I once admitted to my sister during a particularly long memorial service that I thought my brain had broken. This was right after I inexplicably asked her to leave with me during the widow's eulogy so we could get the vanilla milk shake I was suddenly craving. I just couldn't quiet myself. Someone once suggested that I try yoga. "It's healing," she said. "Yoga will help you center yourself and clear your mind." Please. No good could come from pressing my face against a veiny thigh for an hour. I realized it wasn't constructive for me to be alone with my thoughts. Like Michael, I needed constant diversion. Playing tennis or even a pickup game of basketball at our gym required complete concentration and kept my imagination from wandering to the "bad things," as Michael so aptly named them.

After dropping off the kids, I went home and sat at my desk in our cozy office upstairs. Doug's files still hung on their tracks in the bottom drawer. His bow-shaped letter opener and Montblanc pen stood at the ready in the leather penholder. Was every day for the rest of my life going to mean gazing at all the things he'd once touched? Was every morning going to loom as a giant hurdle—a challenge to overschedule the day so I wouldn't feel what I was feeling? All weekend I kept thinking about what Derek said to me—that life was an adventure no matter what the circumstances. I wanted to believe him, but life felt more like a tedious slog than a ride. Still, Derek lodged a thought that maybe I could change my perspective by making a choice I might never have made before.

Before I knew what I was doing, I turned on the computer. "S-T-A-U-B-A-C-H C-O-M-P-A-N-Y," I mouthed as I typed the words into a Google search. I only knew Derek's first name and the name of his firm. Google sent me to Staubach's home page. I clicked on the New York office and entered *Derek* into the company's search engine. One result appeared: Derek Trulson. "Definitely not Jewish," I deduced with a chuckle. I clicked on the link, and Derek's bio appeared. It detailed some of his Seattle deals and mentioned his triathlons and fund-raising efforts for diabetes research. Since I was already in stalker mode, I entered his full name in a new search. The first result was a real estate article he'd cowritten with his former business partner in Seattle. I clicked on it, and a picture of the ridiculously handsome man who stepped on my foot appeared at the top of the article. There he was.

I went back to his bio on the Staubach website and found his work number listed at the top of the page. Should I call him? He'd said he wanted to have coffee sometime. He probably meant after the summer, but what would be the harm in giving him my contact information? Maybe he was right that I should consider spending time with people not directly involved with 9/11. It wasn't as if I wanted to start a relationship. I'd already been on a few "dates," but they were just a way to try to feel normal for a few hours, to get dressed, fill time, get away from my pillow. Derek seemed to offer a similar temporary escape. But making the first call seemed forward. I was raised to believe that the man always did that.

I started to laugh. Rules. What rules? Rules didn't apply to me anymore. I was thirty-five years old with two children and a murdered husband. Gender-role protocols flew out the window. I could do whatever I wanted now. I dialed Derek's number.

He answered on the second ring. "This is Derek."

"Hi, Derek, this is Jennifer Gardner calling. We met at Saracen and—"

"Jennifer! No way. What a surprise," he said with friendly enthusiasm and not a little bit of shock.

"I hope it's okay I called you at the office."

"Of course. How did you find me?"

"Um, well"—I was embarrassed—"I knew your first name and that you worked at Staubach so I, er, googled you."

Derek started laughing. "You're kidding. I don't think I've ever been googled before. Do people really do that?"

"I have no idea what people do, but *I* did. You have to understand, this is uncharted territory. I haven't met a stranger in a bar for over a decade. For all I know you could be a charming pedophile."

"Fair enough. What did you find out? Did you come up with anything interesting?"

"I found the article you wrote with your partner and a few of your triathlon times. Your backstory checked out. I'm impressed with your honesty."

He laughed. "And I'm impressed by your detective work."

I was relieved that Derek seemed happy to hear from me. He could just as easily have been put off by my directness. It struck me, however, that it really didn't matter how I was perceived. It's true that, when the worst happens, you know viscerally that nothing could ever hurt like that again. This knowledge made me feel almost invincible; I didn't care whether someone thought I was too brash. I wanted to reach out to Derek, so I did. I'd been through too much to play games. To my surprise, Derek seemed to appreciate this. He asked me to have a "harmless" dinner that Friday. I accepted, and we exchanged e-mail addresses and cell numbers.

When Friday night arrived, I found myself in my living room in East Hampton waiting for the lights of his car to appear in the driveway. I'd called Allison earlier to discuss wardrobe, and we settled on a sleeveless, navy-blue wrap blouse that tied around the waist with white jeans and heels. I decided to shift my wedding band to my ring finger on my right hand. I wasn't yet ready to take it off, but it felt awkward to wear it that night the traditional way.

Michael and Julia scuttled around the living room, freshly bathed and in their pajamas. Michael was tossing a small rubber basketball into the bright yellow-and-blue plastic hoop I'd inelegantly erected in the center of the living room. Julia was jumping on the couch holding my hands singing "Baby Beluga." It was their bedtime, but I always let them say good-bye at the door when I was going out. They were accustomed to my regular dinners with different "grown-ups"; Derek was just another person I knew. Michael had asked me earlier if Derek was a friend of Daddy's. Without directly addressing his question, I told him that Derek was our friend who'd just moved to New York from Seattle. My children were only five and three—it was better that I didn't categorize the people in our lives as anything but close family friends.

We heard Derek's car pull into the driveway and stop at the stone walkway leading to the front door. "Here we go," I said to myself as Michael and Julia ran to open the door. Derek appeared in the doorway wearing a tan shirt, dark jeans, and black Italian loafers, his thick hair freshly gelled.

"Hi there," Derek said with a dazzling smile.

"Hi, Derek. Please come in."

Derek walked into the small entryway and crouched down to be eye level with the kids. "Hey, guys. I'm Derek. I'll bet you're Michael and Julia." Derek put out his hand for high fives, which my kids delivered with gusto. What could have been a completely awkward moment instead became an adorable mini-playdate. Michael dragged Derek to his basketball hoop, and they started a spirited game of H-O-R-S-E. Julia watched for a while, but she started to yawn and rub her eyes. I took her upstairs to put her to bed while the boys finished their game. Glenda, our sitter, was putting Julia's clean laundry in her closet when we entered the room. I told her I'd left the phone number of the restaurant where we'd be on the kitchen counter. When I came down after reading a few picture books to Julia, Michael was showing Derek his growing basketball-card collection, which he'd spread over the hearth of our fireplace. He scanned his collection for a particular card, then handed it to Derek.

"This is Gary Payton. He plays for Seattle, where you're from."

I could see that Derek was genuinely touched by Michael's gesture. Derek took the card and sat with my son on the couch in front of the fireplace. "This is a special card, Michael. I've watched Gary Payton play for the SuperSonics many times." They looked through a few more cards while Michael shared his detailed analysis of each player's stats. Derek complimented Michael on his prodigious knowledge of basketball arcana, and I silently acknowledged its source. It was time to go. I gave Michael a big squeeze and kissed him on the forehead. Derek thanked him for the game and sharing his card collection. They high-fived once more, and Michael walked us to the door.

······

We drove to Sag Harbor, a scenic historic village on a bay that was once a whaling port and writers' colony. Norah Jones's "Don't Know Why" was playing in Derek's CD player. This was the first time I'd heard her music, and I remember feeling relieved that it didn't trigger any memories. We pulled into the parking lot of B. Smith's restaurant, a Southern-style seafood place overlooking Sag Harbor's famous marina, then went inside to sit at the bar while we waited for our table. I remember Derek tossing his insulin injector in front of him while he ordered a vodka martini and my cosmopolitan, and I asked him if he'd like me to put it in my purse so he wouldn't lose it.

"You're definitely the mother of small children," he said with a wink.

Little did he know I'd reach over and straighten his collar if I could get away with it. I had no idea what I was doing. "I'm sorry. It's instinct. Do you want me to hold the injector?"

"Sure. It's probably safer in your purse. I leave them all over the place."

"No worries. Besides, it is nearly a match for *my* needle." I pulled a large yellow syringe out of my clutch. "Epinephrine. I'm deathly allergic to nuts and carry this EpiPen with me wherever I go."

Derek smirked. "We make an interesting pair."

Eventually, we moved to a table on the deck with views of the marina and harbor. Derek ordered a bottle of wine, and our conversation settled into an easy rhythm. I don't remember everything we talked about over dinner, but I do recall that neither of us ran out of things to say. Derek had a casual manner that made me feel unguarded. That he was drop-dead gorgeous didn't hurt either.

Derek was definitely new to the Hamptons and somewhat flabbergasted by his surroundings. He told me he was living in a "share house"—meaning several strangers split the rent—in Amagansett, a casual ocean village that abuts East Hampton. Shares were always a gamble because one's housemates could be boring, sloppy, cheap, or overgrown fraternity brothers with a penchant for beer pong. Luckily for Derek, he was in a house with fellow triathlon enthusiasts, so early-morning swims and sixty-mile bike rides were the unifying factor.

"We don't have share houses in Seattle. I couldn't believe when my buddy told me to write a check for a few thousand dollars because I 'have to be in the Hamptons.' I had no idea I was buying a tiny room for eight weekends in a dilapidated house."

"Welcome to the upscale South Fork." I smiled. "Everyone at some point in their single days suffers through a share house. Before I met Doug I was in one in West Hampton—twenty-five people in maybe five bedrooms. Cots were lined up in the basement for those who couldn't get an actual room."

"Well, ours isn't that bad. I have to admit, I really like it out here. The Hamptons are not what I expected."

"What did you expect? Saint-Tropez on Long Island?"

"Actually, that's not far off. When I'd hear about the Hamptons, it was always about the crazy parties, spoiled celebrities, and rich people who lived in sprawling mansions with tennis courts and helipads. It's actually more rustic and low-key than I'd imagined. I guess I'm just not going to the right places. Maybe you can show me what I'm missing."

I laughed. "I don't think a barbecue in my backyard with a pool filled with preschoolers wearing yellow floaties is the velvet-rope experience you're looking for."

Time flew by as we chatted. I learned that Derek's ancestors came from Iceland and Norway, which explained Derek's disturbingly Aryan good looks. I chuckled about what a far cry

Scandinavia was from the shtetlach of Russia where my family originated. He asked me whether I was Jewish. I looked at him as if he had three heads. "Isn't it obvious?"

"Hey, I'm just a white boy from the West Coast, what do I know? I knew only two Jewish people in Seattle, and they were twins. I really don't have a religious background. No one in my family is religious, but we do throw the best Christmas parties." I wasn't expecting that answer. I'd just assumed he came from a devout Christian family. I didn't know much about the Pacific Northwest, but Derek looked like the all-American boy to me, complete with Sunday school, red chinos, and Easter-egg hunts.

"Are you Catholic? Protestant?"

"We're a brand of Protestant, I guess," he said with a shrug. "Probably Lutheran, but like I said, we aren't churchgoers. I don't think any of us ever went to church. Are you religious?"

"Well, I'm definitely Jewish," I said emphatically. "I went through the whole training regimen: religious school, bat mitzvah, and was even confirmed. My dad was the president of our synagogue at one time. I don't keep kosher, but I'm about as Jewish as they come." I suddenly realized I was reciting my Jewish credentials as if I were defending my life. Was it really that important to show Derek right then how deep the gulf was between us? Thinking back, I was probably trying to keep him at a safe distance, even though I was the one who googled him.

Derek smiled at me. "Fantastic. I'm not sure I've ever dated a Jewish girl before. See, here's something else you can teach me."

Our conversation turned to how we found ourselves in New York. I told him about my education in Massachusetts and impulsive decision to move to the city. "It happened in the fall of my first year of law school. I spent a weekend in Manhattan with a girlfriend from NYU Law School. After forty-eight hours of exploring the Village, staying out till three in the morning, and meeting a cute guy at a party, I realized that New York was it for me. The day I returned to Cambridge, I withdrew all of my résumés from the Boston firms and sent them to every New York law firm I could name."

Derek laughed. "It's always about a guy, isn't it?"

"Very funny. But, seriously, what twenty-three-year-old could resist the lure of Manhattan?"

Nodding his head, Derek told me he'd had a similar revelation when he made the decision to move East. Derek was in St. Tropez on September 11 to attend the wedding of his college buddy to an English girl. Derek and his friends were on the beach when the planes hit the towers, and they spent the rest of the day glued to the news.

"I'd just been in New York on the ninth during a layover from Seattle. Like everyone else, I couldn't believe what had happened. All those young guys killed in their offices. It drove home for me how short our lives really are. I envied my friend's courage to forgo the expected career route on the West Coast to take a chance on a more fulfilling life in an unfamiliar locale. I'd been contemplating making a change for years, but I never pushed myself to actually do it. I was lazy and comfortable, even though I knew my career was routine and my prospects of getting married and starting a family were dwindling. After the towers fell, I realized that I couldn't wait any longer. I was thirty-five and needed to make a radical change immediately before it was too late. When an opening in Stabauch's New York office presented itself, I jumped. I always loved New York and was amazed at how New Yorkers responded to the attacks with such strength and determination. I couldn't imagine living anywhere else."

I had to smile. September 11 drove so many people out of

New York, but for Derek, it was a siren's call. Even covered in ash, I guess New York was always going to be New York.

"I'll bet it wasn't easy for your family to see you leave the nest."

Derek reddened and rolled his eyes. "My family wasn't thrilled that I was moving, but they *really* were upset with how I broke the news."

"Oh my, what did you do?"

"On Christmas Eve, my family, aunts, uncles, and cousins gathered for dinner and the annual present exchange. When it was my turn to give out gifts, I handed each person an I ♥ NY T-shirt. Everyone nodded in bemused appreciation until my brother, David, asked me why I was giving out New York shirts. I announced with great fanfare that I was leaving Seattle and moving to New York in six weeks. I might as well have taken a shotgun and blown a hole in the ceiling. Everyone was speechless. No one in my family had ever left the Seattle area. They didn't know what to make of me."

"Well, they weren't prepared. At least your parents supported you, right?"

"They didn't know until that moment either," Derek said sheepishly. "My mom was so pissed off. She walked right out of the house and wouldn't speak to me for hours."

I could just imagine my mother's face if I'd pulled a stunt like that. "Are you kidding? You didn't tell your mother first? If I were she, I would've throttled you."

"Apparently, my father, sister, and brother agree with you. I thought it'd be funny, but clearly I was grossly mistaken. It was not one of my better moments as a son."

After dinner, we walked along Main Street, past the historic firehouse, general stores, and ice cream shops to a Thai restaurant for a last drink before ending the evening. Derek and I found a cozy seat in the corner of the tiny lounge and ordered drinks. Looking around the room, he started to compare New York fashion to Seattle's. He told me that he was considered the most fashion-forward of his friends, with a penchant for edgy sunglasses, Italian-cut suits, and bright colors. He definitely had the hallmarks of a metrosexual; I could see it in his gelled hair and pressed jeans. I looked down at Derek's feet.

"You do wear nice shoes, but let me give you a little piece of advice, Mr. Armani. I don't know what they do in Seattle, but in New York men don't wear fine loafers with socks in the summer."

Derek looked gutted. "What do you mean? These are good socks."

"Do you see any other guy wearing socks in here?"

Derek looked around and pointed. "What about that guy over there? He's wearing them."

I giggled. "That man is eighty years old. If you're going for the geriatric look, you've definitely nailed it."

Derek took a sip of his drink, handed me the glass, and started to take off his shoes.

"What are you doing?" I asked warily.

He didn't answer, but took off his socks, put his shoes back on, then stood up and walked to the door. I worried that I'd really insulted him, but then I saw him toss the socks into a trash can next to the entrance. He turned around with a satisfied smirk and triumphantly walked back to our corner with his hands in the air.

"Done," he declared. "No more socks with loafers."

I laughed and laughed: heartily, fully, possibly the first real belly laugh in a long while. And then it hit me—I was laughing. I was enjoying a great, unrestrained evening with a handsome man who wasn't my husband. I wasn't burdened, melancholy, guilty, or even preoccupied; I was buoyant and present and even a little light-headed.

On the way home, Derek asked me to name my favorite places in the Hamptons. One of my top ten was Dreesen's Excelsior Market in East Hampton, the source of the warmest, freshest homemade doughnuts I'd ever had. He asked if I could meet him there the next morning to introduce him to these magical confections while he picked up coffee. I agreed without pausing. I was accustomed to accepting almost any invitation that would fill time. But then I felt a tug of anxiety as I thought about his offer. *What am I doing?* I didn't want to give him the wrong impression. "Jennifer," Derek sensed my hesitation, "it's just coffee and doughnuts. Don't worry."

We pulled into my driveway, and he put the car in park.

"Thanks for a great night." Derek turned to me. "It was nice getting to know you. And thanks for the sock tip."

"Thank you for being patient with me. I know I'm not very good at this, but it was refreshing not to feel like a leper for a few hours."

"You did great. I'll see you tomorrow morning in front of Dreesen's at eight thirty."

He leaned over and gave me a quick peck on the cheek. I felt self-conscious immediately. "Good night, Derek," I said with a feeble wave, got out of the car, and strode as confidently as I could toward the door. When I was halfway up the walk, Derek called out with a laugh, "Jen, my insulin is still in your purse. May I have it back, please?"

12

"I'm so late," I muttered to myself, as I applied the final sweep of mascara to my eyelashes. I looked at my face in the mirror. It was the end of July, a few weeks shy of my thirty-sixth birthday. On the surface, I probably looked like most other women my age—decent skin, a few lines appearing around the eyes, and a figure that owed more to rigorous spin classes and a widow's anxiety than youth and genetics. But I saw something else. My face was still too thin and hollow. I looked weary, like someone who'd completed a grueling journey only to learn that she had to set out again. My eyes betrayed me; no amount of Bobbi Brown concealer and kohl liner could camouflage the strain. Still, every day I thought of my kids as I gamely made up my eyes and brushed some color onto my cheeks. Every day I owed it to them to pull myself together to give them the life they deserved.

Derek was due to pull into the driveway any minute, and I was still in my bathrobe. We had been talking on the phone frequently since our Sag Harbor dinner a few weeks before. He trod so carefully when it came to my situation, gently urging me to seek new experiences that took me out of my everyday 9/11 world. In an e-mail, he offered to be one of the people on whom I could rely for a fun night in the city or a sympathetic ear. I decided to ask him to accompany me to the Orchid Ball in Water Mill, a charity dinner for the Child Development Center of the Hamptons. The CDCH graciously agreed to include a silent auction at the event to benefit the Cantor Fitzgerald Relief Fund. Howard and Allison invited me to be a guest at their table. I thought twice about bringing a date to a public event, but decided it would be liberating to have my own escort instead of being someone's third wheel yet again.

I put the final touches on my lipstick and opened the closet door to get dressed. After several minutes of teenage indecision, I emerged from the carnage of discarded dresses and silky blouses in a simple light green sheath with silver heels, just in time to hear a car engine purr down the driveway.

The Orchid Ball was held on a clear night in a tent on the lush grounds of the Villa Maria, a convent occupying a magnificent white stucco beaux arts mansion located on fourteen acres on a bay in the center of Water Mill. Cocktails and the silent auction were stationed near the tent's entrance, and white tables decorated with orchids—thus the *Orchid* Ball—and a dance floor filled the rest of the space. Women in pastels mingled among men in khakis and sports jackets, as guests started to arrive through a candlelit walkway along the grass. Derek gave me his arm, steering me along the uneven path to a long table of women checking names of guests and providing table numbers. "I'm Jennifer Gardner," I said to the well-coiffed woman holding the clipboard with the guest list. "Gardner, Gardner . . . ," she uttered, flipping through the pages. "Yes, Jennifer Gardner and Derek Trulson.

You're table nine. Enjoy." I will never forget how strange it felt to hear for the first time my name linked with someone's other than Doug's. It sounded foreign, and also, I noted with surprise, not so bad. At least I wasn't alone.

Derek was a deft escort. The minute we walked into the sparkling tent, he commandeered two flutes of champagne from a waiter holding a tray of stemmed glasses. "Let's get the party started," he said with a conspiratorial smile. He walked me over to the hors d'oeuvres stations where sushi, dim sum, and pasta were waiting. "Why don't I hold your drink and purse while you get the food for us?" As instructed, I filled an overflowing plate with a wide selection and fed him tuna rolls and yellowtail sashimi with chopsticks in between my own bites. How many times had I performed this choreography in the past? This was the familiar repertoire of a married couple. I felt normal. For a brief moment, the Scarlet W emblazoned on my chest dimmed just enough for me to blend in with the rest of the crowd.

Allison and Howard appeared at the entrance to the tent just as we finished our first round of sushi. I'd already given them the full download on Derek. They were fully supportive of my new friendship, but also extremely protective of me. I was still fragile and prone to crying jags; my friends were going to make sure any potential companions had genuine intentions. They glided toward us with big smiles and knowing glances. Howard greeted Derek with a hearty clap on the shoulder, but I noticed he had that circumspect look in his eyes, which I remembered from the evening we first met at the Metropolitan Museum. He immediately engaged Derek in conversation, and the two bantered with each other for a while. Allison and I assessed approvingly each other's ensembles, then I pointed out the good food stations (because we both knew that neither of us could relax at these things without eating first).

"How do you feel?" Allison asked while we walked to the buffet table.

"Believe it or not, I'm okay. It's really nice to have someone next to me for a change."

"I'm glad to see you dressed up and smiling."

"I have to admit, though, it's unsettling to see Howard talking with Derek when it should be Doug."

"I know. It's all bizarre. Doug's not here. Gary's not here. We're living in a surreal, upside-down world. Just try to be in the moment, Jen, and let yourself have a good time." Allison always knew when to reel me back from the edge. "Now, pass me one of those plates. Let's eat."

The evening moved from cocktails to dinner to dancing. Early in the evening, Derek and I browsed Cantor's silent auction display—floor seats to a Knicks game, a citrine ring by Judith Ripka, and several golf packages at prestigious Long Island courses. Howard's sister, Edie, and her boyfriend, Lewis Ameri, were chatting with the volunteers behind the tables. Since the attacks, Edie had thrown herself into running the Relief Fund, all the while managing her own bottomless grief over the loss of Gary, her cherished baby brother. She'd arranged for the silent auction to be included at the CDCH's benefit and was planning another fund-raiser on Indian Wells Beach the following week. We hugged across the table. I introduced Derek, and both Edie and Lewis welcomed him kindly.

After dinner, Derek asked me to dance. Before I knew it, he had his arm around my waist, and we were swinging. I've always loved dancing, but that night, my heart hurt as we stepped onto the floor. This didn't feel right. Traditionally, Judaism forbids a person from dancing during the year of mourning—a designated period to remember, heal, and prepare oneself to live with loss. At that moment, I recognized Judaism's prescience. How could I dance? I didn't want to hurt Derek's feelings; he had been working hard all night to make sure I was comfortable and having fun. I waited for the song to end and asked him to walk me back to the table.

The party eventually wound down, and as we headed to the car, I looked at Derek striding next to me and felt pinpricks throughout my body. It reminded me of the sensation one feels when blood flow returns to ice-cold fingers as they warm by a fire. For the last ten months, I'd felt embalmed and wrapped in cotton. Life had become a black-and-white movie, my part played by someone else. Suddenly, I could feel my face flush, a tug in my chest. *Stop thinking, just breathe.*

We drove back to my house, and I invited Derek to come in for a few minutes. The kids were asleep, and only the front entry lights were on. We went to the dark kitchen to raid the refrigerator. I set out a bowl of grapes, some Tate's chocolate chip cookies, and two bottles of water on the island in the center of the room. We devoured everything in sight as if we hadn't eaten all night. Derek looked at his watch, indicating it was time for him to go home. I stood to face him as he leaned against the island.

"I had such a great time," I confessed. "You were a perfect escort."

"It was fun." He nodded. "We'll do it again." He took my hand gently in his.

A stiff silence. Neither of us knew what to do. Derek looked down into my eyes and pulled me into a hug. I rested my cheek on his shoulder, and we stood there for a while, just leaning in. I finally pulled away to find him smiling at me, our faces inches apart. "Is it okay?" he asked. "Yes," I replied, and closed my eyes. He wrapped his arms around my waist and kissed me softly on the lips. There it was. Warmth. Arms. The weight of a man's face on mine. The long-dormant synapses in my brain started to crackle and hiss, like an antique radio coming to life after years on a shelf. I could say that we left it at one, sweet kiss, but the truth is we made out. In my empty kitchen. For more than a little while. Then he tousled my hair as we extricated ourselves from each other, and I walked him to the front door.

I was flustered by the time we kissed good-bye. But Derek just held my face in his hands and said, "You're beautiful. I'll call you tomorrow." I closed the door behind him and literally steadied myself against the frame.

13

I turned thirty-six on August 7. That morning, while I sat in my kitchen watching the *Today* show, it dawned on me that in four more years I would be "older" than Doug. Older than he was when he stopped getting older. And one day he would be gone longer than we were married. This was the sad game of I Spy that I played nearly every day: I Spy my lonely birthday; I Spy Michael's high school graduation; I Spy Julia's wedding. Imagining every milestone Doug would miss made me feel the futility of getting through the day-by-day grind: why aim for normalcy when IEDs were concealed behind every turn of the calendar? It didn't matter if it was six days ago or six years, Doug's death was always going to trip me up, get in the way, tear at my heart. Nothing would ever deaden the ache, and to be honest, I didn't ever want to get to a place where I couldn't feel it sharply.

On this particular birthday morning, I noticed tears dribbling into my bowl of Special K. *Get it together, Jen.* Pam and her husband, Matt, were hosting a small birthday dinner for me at a local

Wainscott restaurant, Ristorante Capri. Of course, they'd been at the party Doug threw the year before in our new house, and they knew this first birthday without him would be grim.

Pam continued to be a lifesaver that first year—she registered Julia for ballet, forced me out of bed to meet her for coffee, insisted I join her pals for girls' nights out. She always seemed to intuit what would help get me through a day. I didn't want to mark my birthday; there was nothing to celebrate. Pam convinced me to let her put a dinner together anyway. "Jennifer, your friends want to be there for you. We want to be there for us, too. Consider it selfish— we've all been through so much this year. Trust me, it'll be fine."

That night, I drove the short distance to the restaurant on Montauk Highway. Pam and Matt had reserved a long table in the back. Among the couples already mingling, I saw Allison and Howard talking to the Weinbergs. *This is a safe room.* I chided myself for always anticipating the worst. Pam was right, the dinner was a good idea. I walked over and put my head on her shoulder. "Hi, everybody. A little widow birthday party, anyone?"

Pam rolled her eyes. "You're so ridiculous. Isn't this nice? I told you it would be okay."

I put my hands up in defeat. "You were right. I admit I've been looking forward to this all day."

A waiter took my drink order, and I settled into light conversations. Eventually, Pam pulled me aside and asked furtively about Derek.

"So, what's going on? I heard you had fun at the Orchid Ball. Have you heard from him since?"

"Funny you should ask. This morning, a basket of flowers arrived at my door. His note said, 'Happy Birthday. Look forward to your life's adventure. Love, Derek.'"

"Wow. All from a guy who stepped on your foot in a bar."

I laughed. "My life is a Lifetime movie."

"At least you're smiling. Do you like him?"

"You mean, *like* him like him?"

Immediately Pam and I were giggling teenagers. "Of course that's what I mean."

I didn't really know what to say. To actually "*like* him like him" would topple the wobbly rationale I'd constructed to justify Derek's presence. I was still Doug's wife; Derek was just a sweet trifle, an occasional pleasant diversion.

"I don't know. He's a nice guy, but right now I just want to pass the time without thinking about anything deeper than what shoes to wear. I'm not sure I'm even capable of liking someone to the point where it matters if I ever saw the person again. Honestly, Pam, just having a small semblance of a personal life is refreshing enough."

"It sounds like this is just what you need for now. I'm happy for you. When are you going to see him again?"

"He's coming over tomorrow with his friend Rodney to play basketball with Michael. I think he may like my kids more than he likes me, which works just fine."

"You're kidding. Is it strange to have him with the kids?"

"Actually, not at all. It's not like he's my boyfriend or anything, God forbid. Michael and Julia are so used to spending time with guys like Howard and Uncle Scott that they think every adult male is a playdate."

"Well, here's to a personal life," Pam said, clinking my glass. "Let's go sit down and toast your birthday."

.....

It was as if someone set an egg timer the minute my birthday passed. The countdown had started, and I could hear the *tick*,

tick wherever I was. I was entering the end-of-summer weeks that, one year ago, were Doug's last. I knew what was coming: The same air before he died. The same light. The same rhythm of days as beach afternoons bled into fall jackets. It had been a restful summer, but now I was twitchy again.

I jammed our days with sports for the kids, ice cream excursions into town, and a major cellar reorganization project. All of Doug's things that I saved from the city were stuffed into large, black garbage bags piled at the bottom of the basement stairs. With armloads of storage containers from Kmart, I set to work hanging Doug's clothing in garment bottom, wrapping his tuxedo shoes, loafers, and stiff basketball sneakers in chamois cloths, and stacking his papers, record albums, and mementos in plastic boxes on new metal shelves that I put together a few days earlier with Doug's new tools he'd barely touched. Going through everything, I wished I had Doug's watch—I'd given it to him for our fifth anniversary. He wore it to work that day, and now it was dust.

I placed two large storage boxes—labeled *9/11 stuff*—on the top shelves, far out of reach. They contained newspaper clippings, memorial programs, and reams of sympathy cards and letters. Vicky and Pam's comically inadequate guest book from the memorial service, stuffed with the extra legal-pad pages, lay in one box next to Doug's battered credit and identification cards, which were still encased in the plastic evidence bag from One Police Plaza—the only tangible evidence I had that proved Doug actually died. On top of those souvenirs, I'd laid a certificate I received from NASA bearing a piece of an American flag that had been flown in space in memory of the 9/11 victims.

Putting things in order helped me cope with the brimming resurgence of Doug's last days in the Hamptons. What also helped was a small but touching gesture from one of Doug's basketball buddies, Bill Frischling. Billy and Doug were friends from their grade school days on Fire Island. He was another giant like Doug, and the two of them played together in more city leagues and tournaments than I could count. Billy played in the first game ever hosted at our house the previous summer and witnessed Doug's inaugural shot. He wanted to honor Doug in some way, not just for him, but for Michael and Julia, who were clearly showing early signs of Doug's athletic ability.

Billy called in July to ask if he could hold a memorial "run" at our court on the August anniversary of that first game. I was thrilled; Michael and Julia would see that Daddy's friends remembered him. The games were competitive and exciting, with Doug's friends from different playgrounds and gyms coming together to put on a show for our kids. Even Howard and Uncle Scott played. Michael and Julia handed out Gatorade like pros, while I marveled at how nice it felt to be among the "tall" guys again.

Billy promised to do it the next year and has held the annual Doug's Run on our court every August for the past ten years. The guys have obviously aged a bit, and the Ace bandages, Advil, and metal knee braces have multiplied, but the old warriors continue to play their eleven-point matches on Doug's court every summer. The best part: Michael recently started playing point guard in the games and has frequently hit the three just like his dad.

August ended, and it was suddenly the first of September— the final days approaching without a moment to prepare. When the calendar flipped, I slipped my armor back over my shoulders like a familiar cardigan. I was already feeling apprehensive about having to pack up the house and kids by myself to make the lonely transition back to the city. God certainly had a warped sense of timing. Wasn't September stressful enough with crazed back-to-school shopping, new schedules, and the High Holidays around the corner? I know it sounds glib, but couldn't the terrorists have picked January or February when city life was quiet under gray slush and freezing temperatures?

Michael's first day of kindergarten was September 11, and for the rest of my children's academic careers, their first days of school would be marred by stark reminders and public memorials driving home the undeniable reality that their father was murdered that week however many years ago.

The kids and I piled into our jammed SUV on September 7 and headed back to the city. I was looking forward to showing Michael and Julia their new rooms. During the summer, the contractors had nearly completed the renovation, and each of us had a fresh new bedroom. Julia was delighted with her pink-and-yellow princess room with its cushioned reading nook, shelves teeming with Beanie Babies and girly bedside lamps with crystal shades. Her bedroom shared a narrow tiled bathroom with Michael's blue-and-white, basketball-themed room. A plastic Knicks hoop hung prominently on his closet door, and framed posters of Michael Jordan and Patrick Ewing graced the white walls on either side of his red trundle bed. My bedroom was still a mess of exposed wires, sawdust, and drywall; I would bunk in the guest room for the next five weeks until it was finished. Though moving into a construction site was hardly ideal, at least we weren't coming home to the same melancholy rooms where Doug said his final good-byes.

The first anniversary arrived with a Windex-blue sky and the sound of traffic humming along Central Park West. It was 7:00 a.m.; one year ago, I was joking with Doug by his closets as he got dressed. Today, I was taking Michael to his first day of kindergarten with my mother and attending another Cantor memorial service in Central Park. When I woke up that morning, I thought the day might not be too bad. The weeks of anticipation had been the hard part—today was really just another day in the long continuum of days without my husband. I was armed and ready, or so I thought.

Later, after returning from Michael's school in Riverdale, I sat on my unmade bed and watched the ceremonial reading of the names at Ground Zero, which I'd taped earlier. The speakers solemnly announced each name in alphabetical order as photos of smiling young men and women appeared at the bottom of the screen. It was interminable, like a slow stream of water that, over time, bores a hole through bedrock. I looked up at the ceiling and silently thanked Doug for having the forethought to be born a Gardner and not a Zerbowski. The *F*'s turned to *G*'s, and I waited for his turn, pulling the loose comforter tighter around my frame. I thought it would be anticlimactic; it wasn't as if I didn't know what was coming. Then I heard it. My husband's name emerging from a stranger's mouth. To hear "Douglas Benjamin Gardner" among the tragic roll call staggered me. I wailed like a wounded animal, impaled on each syllable of his name. How was I going to get through this day?

After fast-forwarding to catch some of our friends' names— Goldflam, Gooding, Gurian, Kates, Kirwin, Lutnick, Richards, Shea, Varrachi—I dragged myself down the hallway to my desk and sat in front of the computer. Several months earlier, Howard asked me to be one of the featured speakers at the memorial service, and I needed to make some last-minute changes to my speech. For weeks, I'd vacillated over whether to participate. I struggled to write something that would resonate with the families, but every time I tried to describe our "long journey" or "strength as a community," I bored even myself. The last thing anyone wanted to hear was a litany of clichés and tired metaphors on a day when everyone really just felt like hiding under the covers to wait out the hours. After watching Michael courageously address his classmates that morning, any doubts I had about speaking evaporated. If Michael could take ownership of the day, so could I. Maybe that was the message: we didn't have a choice about what had happened to us, but we could choose how to live with it.

Jayme and Scott arrived at the apartment to take me to the service. My sister hugged me. "Do you remember that first night when you begged for it to be a year from now? It is. You made it. I'm so proud of you." I shrugged and reminded her she might want to hold off on the mazel tovs. About eight hours were still left in the day. My parents stayed behind to take care of the kids until I returned. Walking through Central Park toward those same iron gates catapulted me back to the first October memorial. Except this time, reporters and television cameras were stationed several deep outside the registration tables to catch attendees as they walked past. A local television reporter stopped the three of us and asked how we felt on that first anniversary of 9/11. "I don't think we ever move on from this kind of loss," I volunteered into the microphone. "We just continue to move through it. I think the best we can do is slap a smile on our faces when necessary and hope that, one day, our insides catch up with our outsides."

Jayme squeezed my hand. "Perfect. Always the achiever, aren't you?" I punched her in the arm. Like last year, I took my seat in the front row with Allison to my left and Jayme and Scott to my right. This time I didn't retreat from Allison; I hugged her tightly instead and entwined my arm with hers as we waited for the program to begin. I waved to Pam, Vicky, and their husbands, who found seats near the back; we were having dinner later to put an emphatic period on the day with comfort food and several bottles of good wine. The service would be nearly identical to the last one: the same chevron of white chairs under a tent, flag-draped stage, and the Harlem Boys Choir sitting on risers. Howard walked over to us and asked me to follow him; I was the first speaker, and he wanted me sitting on the stage until I delivered my speech. I walked up the stairs to where Stuart Fraser, once again the master of ceremonies, waved for me to sit near the lectern. We embraced before I sat down, and he flashed me his familiar mischievous smile that calmed my nerves.

Hillary Clinton, who was then a New York senator, walked out and sat in the chair next to me. I don't care on which side of the aisle you sit, Senator Clinton was by far the most effective and loyal advocate for New York following the attacks. She pushed the Red Cross to distribute critically needed funds to victims' families and joined with our intrepid New York legislators to fight for federal funding to rebuild lower Manhattan. While some politicians were busy rebranding 9/11 as their personal resurrection stories, Hillary worked heroically on behalf of *all* the families—rescue workers and "civilians." She never abandoned Cantor Fitzgerald even when the media gorged on false, mean-spirited portraits of Howard.

After the invocation and the Boys Choir's renditions of the national anthem and "God Bless America," I walked to the microphone. Like Michael, I needed to make an impact today, to take back some control over events that had left me powerless. September 11 happened to me; I couldn't allow myself to be swept away by the anniversary like a flimsy leaf on a raging river. The wind suddenly whipped violently across the stage. The tents swayed, and the bunting flapped loudly. One could barely hear my amplified voice above the whooshing of swirling air. No one missed the obvious symbolism.

Someone once asked whether I thought Doug was at peace. I didn't think so. If anything, I imagined he was furious and pacing back and forth across heaven's equivalent of a hardwood floor, frustrated that he wasn't able to finish what he started. I knew that wherever Doug was could not possibly be a "better place"; home with his children was Doug's sacred ground. I silently implored my husband to take a breather and allow his wife to finish her speech in peace. As in life, he only pretended to listen, and the wind continued to buffet the stage.

I looked down at the words I'd written and started to speak. I talked about how grieving isn't linear. "We don't just 'get better' as time goes on . . . we vacillate between hope and despair, strength and weakness, the belief that we can get through this and then an unforgiving recognition that life will never be the same." I talked about losing Doug in such a public way and how we would always be the families of the victims of 9/11. But I also said that life was good, despite the evidence to the contrary. I told the audience how humbled I was by the outpouring of love and support from our families, community, and Cantor. I wished everyone peace in their memories and asked that God bless us all "because, if I may be so bold, quite frankly, we deserve it." I wish I could say that my soaring rhetoric moved the crowd to tears, but honestly, it was about as impressive as a steaming bowl of canned soup. I was just happy to hit my marks and get off the stage, though I did earn a nice embrace from Senator Clinton while the audience clapped politely.

I don't remember much of the rest of the service, other than LaChanze singing "I Will Remember You" at its conclusion. She was magnificent; her haunting, resonant voice left everyone reaching for Kleenex. Her eleven-month-old daughter, Zaya, rested peacefully in her grandmother's arms while Celia, the three-year-old, watched her mother perform with rapt attention. Celia was a miniature version of Calvin, and she greeted me after the service with the same fierce hug and heart-stopping smile her father always gave me.

I missed my friends. Had it really been a year since I'd heard Calvin's laugh or teased my raffish friend Gary Lutnick about finding a nice girl to marry? It seemed like a lifetime ago, but on second look, it felt like yesterday. Were our lost friends really reduced to ghostly memories, brief montages of nostalgic reminiscences? When I concentrated on Doug, I tried to see him bodily, hear his voice, recall full afternoons with the kids at the park. Sometimes I could freeze the moment, but mostly it was like trying to hold water in my hands. LaChanze and I talked about how at the one-year anniversary we felt like Dr. Doolittle's Pushmi-pullyu, stuck in place as yesterday and tomorrow tugged us in opposite directions.

I reflected on the reporter's question from earlier when I answered that we never really move on from this kind of loss. I hated to admit it, but we all had come a long way since the night I begged Jayme to fast-forward my life. A few days before the anniversary when I was bathing Michael, he asked if I remembered the time when I "couldn't play"—those first awful months when I rarely left my room. He told me he used to hide by my bedroom door and listen to me cry on the telephone. "I'm glad you're not like that anymore, Mommy," he said. "You play with us now and can give me a bath." In a year, I went from shattered to functional, the only gift I could give him and his sister that mattered. I was thankful for that, but I also found myself looking forward to things on the calendar. I was excited about Jayme and Scott's wedding in November; they'd pared down their originally scheduled March affair to a simple civil service because of the attacks. Now they were having a real wedding ceremony and reception, and I was surprised how glad I was to perform my matron-of-honor duties. Nothing was more important than giving Jayme and my brother-in-law the celebration they so deserved.

I have to confess that my thoughts also drifted to Derek. He called me after Doug's name was read that morning at Ground Zero. He wanted me to know that he'd watched for it, and then, poor thing, he listened with quiet compassion to my barely coherent, sobbing elegy for my husband. Derek had taken me to a movie the night before to get my mind off the day to come. It never ceased to astound me that a strapping man from the West Coast, who could be enjoying the company of much less complicated and wildly more attractive younger women, was choosing instead to help me pick up the pieces of my life. What was even more alarming was that I was starting to like his company more than I wanted to admit. Derek made me feel normal, whatever that meant post-9/11, and I got a secret charge every time I saw his name pop up on my BlackBerry. Not only wasn't he threatened by my loss—and my obvious devotion to a man who was gone—but Derek allowed me my ongoing struggle and even tried to share in Doug's memory with me.

After the movie, Derek asked if I wanted him to come to the memorial service. He said, "I'll do whatever feels good for you. Just know that I'm here in whatever way you need me." I was torn. On the one hand, it was important that Derek grasp the magnitude of the tragedy by witnessing the sea of family members gathered to remember Cantor's fallen 658. However, the mere idea of bringing an escort to the first anniversary of my husband's death—even if Derek sat in the back—was unthinkable. So I said no. I needed to stand alone and mark the last time I saw my beautiful Douglas alive.

It was the right decision. I knew I still wasn't ready to be anything other than Doug's wife. I looked down at the eternity band on my ring finger, which Doug had grandly presented to me a few days after Julia was born to celebrate our new daughter. Exhaling a sigh of defeat, I whispered to my absent husband, "See, Doug. I made it through the year. You can come back now."

14

Once the anniversary passed, life continued—routine was its own salve. I loaded Michael on the bus to Riverdale every morning, with his enormous blue backpack hoisted on his skinny shoulders nearly engulfing him. "It's not heavy, Mom," he'd say, exasperated, as I tried to adjust the straps. "I can do it." He was separating from me a little better now. He liked the bus drill; it was comforting for him to know the time he had to be ready and what time the bus would arrive at school and home in the afternoon. He'd only get rattled if there was traffic. The fear of being late or my not knowing where he was could paralyze him. I asked Michael once, "What's the worst that could happen if you were late?"

"What if no one could find me?" he answered. I couldn't fault his logic.

Julia was in her second year of preschool. Every morning, I joined the cattle drive of parents in workout gear or business suits as we waited in the school's lobby for the doors of the ancient elevator to open and carry us with our sleepy charges to the classrooms. Though it was still jarring for me to walk the yellow hallways amid the cubbies and papier-mâché sculptures where I'd first learned of Doug's death, at least Julia felt safe here. She'd bound out of my arms and rush into her classroom, straight to the sand table or painting easels.

Julia was a pistol, a tiny, self-contained hurricane of energy. I was aware of feeling both relief and sorrow that she wouldn't remember her father. She wouldn't actually miss him, and that would spare her trauma, but she wouldn't have any memories of the man who adored her, and that was heartbreaking. I would have to give her my memories of her daddy. I'd tell her how I remembered his large hands under her arms, as he tossed her in the air in her striped bathing suit. Or the way he nuzzled her until she dissolved in a fit of giggles. She had to know that my favorite images were Daddy kissing her when she first emerged at Mount Sinai hospital, and him wrapping her in a lion towel after her bath, the two of them roaring in the mirror like Simba and Mufasa. Somehow I'd give Julia her father, even if it meant inundating her with my hand-me-down memories until she could recite the anecdotes verbatim.

I was adjusting to my role as a single parent, but it seemed I was auditioning for another part as fall turned to winter: girlfriend. Derek and I began seeing each other regularly once the anniversary passed. I don't know how it happened, but it seemed every time we made a plan, two more would follow. Dinners, drinks in SoHo, a walk around the reservoir in Central Park—we explored the city like tourists, which, indeed, in a way, we were. The mood in New York had indelibly shifted after 9/11. Of course, Manhattan was back to business as usual, but one could sense an unease permeating everyday life. People were subdued, more cautious about taking subways and buses. Large gatherings at public venues gave way to more intimate dinners and cocktail parties in people's apartments. The city was sobered, wary, and I felt like an alien walking along the sidewalk holding hands with Leif Eriksson.

Since Derek lived a mere three blocks away, it was easy to have a spontaneous after-work drink or catch a late movie at the nearby cinema. Some weekday evenings, he would ask to stop by to say hello and play with the kids. Michael looked forward to their frequent one-on-one games of bedroom basketball. Julia, my little imp, flirted with him as only a three-year-old could. She'd cover Derek with her stuffed-animal collection and thrust books in his hand whenever he sat down. She sees Derek as a toy just like Daddy, I thought, watching Julia wrap her pajama-clad shape around Derek's long leg one evening. Derek was delightful with my kids—silly and attentive, but never overstepping his bounds.

I still saw Derek as a respite from my "real" life. With him, I could temporarily suspend the daily battle with anxiety and loneliness and simply be. He was fun, uncomplicated, and didn't ask me for anything. He was just as happy as I was not to define our "relationship." I couldn't fathom the idea of seriously dating anyone, and Derek was firmly a bachelor trying to establish himself in a new city. Still, we were inexplicably gathering steam. Kissing him made me loopy. I couldn't wait to feel his arms around me and melt into his shoulders, neck, and chest. It was a delicious sensation that made me hungry for more, but I was on my guard. I'd actually become aware of how dangerous loneliness could be; I'd seen other widows make unfortunate choices in their desperation to get out from under the gloom. They confused revived desire with affection, though who could blame them? To have been married and then instantly condemned to a numbed, contactless existence left one somewhat ill-equipped to navigate a new flirtation. I was adamant that I would not fall into that trap.

One late-summer night, Derek and I spent a spirited evening having cocktails on the terrace lounge at the trendy Hudson Hotel. The place was like an urban Garden of Eden with love seats and private corners tucked into lush plants and flowers everywhere. Derek and I sprawled on a love seat fashioned from a converted wheelbarrow and canoodled until the bartender announced last call. I didn't want the night to end and expected Derek to feel the same. So I was caught short when Derek walked me to my door, pecked me on the cheek, and said good night.

"Excuse me," I said, blinking my eyes rapidly. "What just happened?"

Derek gave a wry smile. "It's late. I'll see you tomorrow night after work."

I was suddenly embarrassed. Did I do something wrong? Misread every signal?

"Okay . . . ," I began unsteadily. "I don't know what's going on, but if you have to go, good night."

Derek chuckled; his amusement at my discomfort rattled me. "Jennifer, you're something else. I can tell you're not used to people saying no to you," he said.

I rolled my eyes. "Derek, for nearly the last decade I've been a sure thing. Forgive me if I don't know how to do this properly."

Derek just laughed again. "Go to bed. I'll see you tomorrow."

The next night, Derek and I met for dinner at a midtown restaurant near his office. We sat across from each other in a long booth, both of us uncharacteristically quiet. I could tell Derek had something to say. I suspected he was going to announce that we should stop seeing each other. I figured that the ramifications of pursuing a relationship with a recently widowed mother were probably too much. I had to give him credit for hanging in as long as he had.

Like most women, I've been on the receiving end of a breakup, and no matter how awful the relationship, it always stung. But as I sat in front of Derek waiting for him to speak, I was aware that the idea of never seeing him again didn't really bother me. I guess that's the residual damage from catastrophic loss: once you've been through the worst, everything else seems inconsequential.

"Jennifer, I think we should talk about last night."

"It was pretty awkward. I think I totally misread the situation."

"You didn't misread anything. It's just that I didn't feel comfortable staying with you until we talked about it."

"What do you mean by 'it'?"

"I mean that I'm not sure you're—ready," he said carefully, trying to choose the right words. "I think you're still fragile, and maybe we should take this more slowly. I don't want you to get swept away by something you'll regret later."

Wait a minute, I thought to myself. Who was he to tell me who I am? That he was echoing my own concerns was immaterial and, frankly, somewhat annoying. I didn't like that he saw through my bravado, forcing me to verbalize how precarious the next steps could be for me. In truth, I didn't want to think anymore. We could worry about the ramifications in the morning.

"I'm not 'swept away' by you, Derek. I'm really just enjoying our new friendship/relationship, whatever you want to call it. It's easy and, as you suggested, takes me out of my life for a while. I think I can handle this. Do you think, perhaps, you can't? Maybe you're trying to let me down gently? I can understand that my package deal might not be what you envisioned for yourself."

Derek gave me a hard look. "Where would you get that idea? If I wanted to stop seeing you, I'd just tell you. Your situation doesn't frighten me; I just want to be respectful. I'm very attracted to you—obviously. To be honest, this is the first truly adult relationship I've had in a long time, and I like it. I just don't want to hurt you. I'm still new here in New York, and I'm not looking to get married or even think about that anytime soon."

I nearly fell over. "Derek, are you kidding? Do you honestly think I'm interested in a serious relationship, let alone marriage? I don't even want to admit to anyone that I'm seeing you. I know I sound hypocritical, but I still feel married to Doug. I'm just putting one foot in front of the other, and you've played a big part in helping me do that. I'm grateful, but I assure you I'm not looking for you or anyone to rescue me with a diamond ring and a new last name."

Now it was Derek's turn to be embarrassed. "Well, um, I didn't really think you wanted to get married. I just thought we should be clear with each other before we decided to take things further. I don't want you to think I'm a player or anything. I'm just not ready for a real commitment. How could I be—I'm still living with two roommates in a glorified dorm room for God's sake. I'm a good guy, I promise, and I simply don't want to do anything that could hurt you."

I looked at my handsome date, stammering his feelings to me over a vodka martini. This was the most peculiar conversation I'd ever had with any man. For most single women, Derek's non-committal attitude would have been a deal-breaker, but for me, it was a godsend. That he also didn't know any of my friends was an additional bonus, making it much easier for me to enjoy our time together without guilt. For the first time in a long time, I was going to have a private life.

"I appreciate your honesty, but if it's okay with you, I'd rather not define or discuss our 'relationship' to death. Why don't we just agree to continue whatever this is and allow it to grow or fizzle on its own?"

"I can handle that," Derek replied with relief. "I think the less we say about 'us' the better."

"I agree. There is one thing, however, that I will need if we're going to move forward." I figured this was the time to ask for final concessions as negotiations were coming to a close. "If we do sleep together at some point, I have to insist on monogamy. I can't even believe I'm saying this, but I'm too old to wonder whether I'm just one of a harem. If you're interested in seeing other women, please just tell me so I can extricate myself with a modicum of dignity."

Derek shook his head and smiled. "Jennifer, you don't ever have to worry about that. I told you I'm a good guy—a one-woman-at-a-time guy. You have my word."

This was getting interesting. It wasn't as if I were falling in love; maybe he could just be the "sorbet" between courses—a sweet bridge to carry me to my newly unattached life. I just needed to keep him contained in this defined role for my plan to work.

"I'm so glad we met. You've made me feel like a normal girl—no small feat. What a surprise this has been. Like you said, life is an adventure."

We finished dinner, paid the bill, and headed for the door. Instead of going home, we drove to the Lowell Hotel, a charming boutique hotel on the East Side. I was nervous and could barely look the concierge in the eye when Derek and I walked through the tiny lobby and checked in. I shouldn't have been so self-conscious; I was an experienced adult. But Derek wasn't my husband, and it felt illicit.

Although our "first time" was anything but spontaneous, it was memorable nonetheless. I guess you could say it was like riding a bicycle, but a lot more fun than pedaling a Schwinn. I still smile when I recall what he whispered in my ear when we finally disentangled ourselves: "Oh, boy, Jennifer, you're going to be trouble."

15

"Are you ready to be unveiled?" I asked Derek as we stepped out of the taxi on Lafayette Street into the cool October air. It was Allison's birthday, and she and Howard had invited several couples to dinner at Butter, an of-the-moment downtown restaurant, where occasionally the Olsen twins and other young celebrities congregated. Up until that night, Derek and I had kept our relationship mostly on the down-low to allow me—and everyone in my life—time to acclimate. This would be our first public coming-out, and Derek was about to meet a tableful of Doug's closest friends.

"Absolutely," he said as we walked to the door. "Are you?"

"I'm nervous. This is a protective group. They're going to love you, but just be prepared. They might grill you."

"Don't worry about me. They can ask me anything."

We headed through the airy upstairs restaurant to the staircase in the back that led down to the Birch Room, a darker, more intimate dining area where the walls and ceiling were lined with silver-birch branches. Elise and Stuart Fraser were there, along with LaChanze and several of Allison's friends from high school. Before I could take a breath, Derek immediately walked over to the Frasers, introduced himself, and launched into a friendly conversation. From their body language, I could tell Elise and Stuart didn't know what to make of the stunning WASP who was engaging them, but within seconds I could see them relax. Derek had a gift for drawing people in; one could argue it was the salesman training or his West Coast charisma, but I knew Derek's congeniality sprang from a sincere desire to get to know people. New York was full of self-advertisers who wanted to trumpet their own achievements on first meeting, but not Derek. He asked questions and really listened to the answers.

When Howard and Allison arrived, a quiet celebration began. They sat Derek between LaChanze and me. It had been a difficult year for her—especially with the birth of Zaya a month after the attacks—but she was beginning to find her footing again. She'd recently accepted a role in an off-Broadway production of *The Vagina Monologues*, which Allison, Elise, and I were planning to see in a few weeks. Though she wasn't dating, LaChanze confided she was starting to think about it. I'd already told Derek the history of our friendship with her and Calvin, which gave him the impetus to turn his full attention to her through appetizers and most of dinner. I saw LaChanze smiling and laughing. When Derek eventually turned to talk with others at the table, she leaned toward me.

"Oh my God, Jennifer. He's amazing. And *adorable*."

"Well, I guess if God was going to make me start over, the least He could do was give me something nice to look at."

"You got that right," she giggled. "But, seriously, he seems to be a genuinely nice guy. He asked me a ton of questions about Calvin and my daughters. He wanted to know how I was coping and how it felt seeing you with him. What was most interesting was that he really wanted me to know how much he respected you."

"I'm relieved you like him. I think this is harder for Derek than he lets on. I'm sure he didn't plan to catapult from Seattle into the epicenter of 9/11."

"He's wearing it well. When I asked how it was for him to sit at this loaded table, he told me he was more concerned with how everyone else felt. He didn't want anyone to be uncomfortable around him."

"That's nice to hear. We'll see what happens. He's a welcome distraction."

"I'll toast to that."

The dinner ended, and we all gathered around the bar. I couldn't help but worry about what Allison and Howard really felt about having Derek at their table. We'd fallen into a relatively comfortable dynamic with me as their plus-one. Maybe I was overthinking things, but I worried whether it hurt them to watch their best friend's widow become romantically attached to another man. I took Allison aside when we went to the ladies' room.

"How do you think Derek did tonight?" I asked while we reapplied lip gloss at the mirrors.

"I think everyone had a great time," she said. "Derek is so easy to be around."

"I hope you didn't mind having him here. Are you sure you're okay with him and me?"

Allison looked at me squarely. "I've never given it a second thought. You have to live. I'm behind you one hundred percent."

"I know, but I worry about it being too painful. What does Howard think?"

"Honestly? Do you know what he always says whenever anyone asks that question? Every time it comes up he answers, 'If Jennifer's happy, I'm happy.' You're not just Doug's wife to us. Doug was our best friend, but you are, too. We love you, and we're in it with you for life, like it or not."

I shouldn't have been surprised by Allison's and Howard's reaction. They reminded me that Doug existed, mattered, and would always be missed. But they also wanted me to have another chapter. I think they were planning for my future long before I ever believed I'd have one. During the early stages of my apartment renovation, I showed Howard drawings of the proposed master bedroom. When Howard mentioned that I'd included only one bathroom sink, he shook his head and insisted I add a second one.

"Howard, you know I don't need another sink. It's just me here."

"Think of it as a good investment," came his glib response. "A second sink will increase the value of the apartment for resale."

"I'm not selling this apartment, ever."

"Fine, but you need two sinks anyway. People like two sinks."

"I know what you're doing, my friend," I said, wagging my finger. "There isn't ever going to be another person brushing his teeth next to me."

Howard pointed to the drawing. "I know you think that now, but one day there will be. And he's going to want to shave in peace."

"Enough already." I was starting to get agitated. "I'm *never* going to be with anyone ever again. The thought of it is unbearable. One sink."

Howard chuckled watching me disintegrate. "Okay, okay." He put up his hands in mock defeat. "No other men. But put the sink in for me. Every Men's Night Out I'm going to come over and wash my face in it."

⋯⋯

I wish I could say Derek and I enjoyed only smooth sailing in the beginning, but postmarriage relationships are complicated enough without a national tragedy added to the mix. It was one thing for me to dip a toe into romance, but quite another to watch my children grow closer to him. Of course, I was thrilled that Derek earnestly pursued a friendly but respectful relationship with my kids, but it sometimes hurt to see them play so effortlessly. Every interaction was a razor-sharp reminder of what Doug was missing.

On Halloween, I remember Julia running to Derek and begging him to carry her after a long night of trick-or-treating on West Sixty-Eighth Street. She was a damsel in a purple gown with a sparkly tiara, and Michael was her knight in ersatz chain mail. We were walking the festive street with Doug's parents, who Derek had just met for the first time. Joe and Charlotte were extraordinary that emotionally charged evening; whatever trepidation or uneasiness they might have had about meeting my new companion, they concealed it elegantly behind animated smiles and warm handshakes. But, when Derek hoisted Julia's little body onto his shoulders, I gasped. It was beautiful to see Julia delightedly making a mess of Derek's meticulously gelled hair and hearing her laugh as he pretended to stumble. But I couldn't look. He was doing Doug's job. I was instantly unsteady and could only imagine how Joe and Charlotte must have felt, watching their granddaughter held aloft by a tall, young man who wasn't their son.

I wasn't the only one who harbored contradictory feelings about Derek's deepening connection to Michael and Julia. Some of Doug's friends were struggling to accept it, too. No matter how carefully I defined my relationship with Derek, I couldn't put the brakes on my children's increasing affection.

At Brandon Lutnick's birthday party in January 2003, it became clear to me that Michael's and Julia's open affection for Derek would be the most difficult hurdle. Brandon's party was held on the Intrepid Sea, Air & Space Museum, a historic aircraft carrier that was converted to a museum with function rooms for private events. It was a typical Sunday-afternoon scene of moms and dads trying to manage their overstimulated young children while simultaneously attempting to complete two consecutive sentences to a fellow adult in the room. The kids darted from the snack table to the arts-and-crafts projects, never stopping for more than a minute before something new caught their attention. The room was filled with the familiar gathering of the Lutnicks' friends and family—with the exception of Doug and Gary, whose absence still hadn't become routine even after a year.

Derek arrived late and walked in amid the chaos. Michael and Julia saw him enter and squealed in unison, "Derek!" They rushed to him and jumped into his waiting arms, as if this were a routine honed over many years. Doug's friends quieted to take in the surreal picture, then quickly covered their astonishment by turning back to whatever they were doing. Derek noticed the sudden drop in temperature, but continued to hug and high-five the kids enthusiastically as if nothing had happened. I adored him for that; Derek didn't want Michael and Julia to think they were doing anything wrong. As for the rest of us, how could we not notice Doug's children leaping into another man's arms? I tried to stifle my unease. I looked around the room—it was filled with daddies. Michael and Julia were the only ones without a father, and at that moment Derek was a welcome substitute. Still, I couldn't help thinking, "Wrong guy." It killed me that it wasn't Doug loving his children. But who could deny how secure and happy they were to have a man who belonged to them? I walked over to Allison. "Did you see that?"

She replied, "I always see that. And I always know you do, too. Just breathe."

Elise and Stuart Fraser were also at the party. Elise's brother's death in the towers had unhinged her equilibrium and sent her reeling. While I sat in my bedroom watching reruns of sitcoms or *Sesame Street* videos with Julia, Elise coped by watching the Food Network even though she didn't really cook. She also explored Buddhism and psychic readings to try to make sense of the loss. We talked every few days, propping each other up and comparing notes on our sometimes preposterous forays into various healing strategies. I confessed to Elise my ambivalence about the kids' interactions with Derek. She tried to reassure me that my feelings were valid, and also noted that no one had a playbook for this kind of thing. After the birthday party, she told me that her eleven-year-old daughter Samantha was also troubled by how demonstrative my children were with Derek. Samantha feared I'd replaced Doug, and Michael and Julia had forgotten their father. Elise told me her daughter worried that Elise would have replaced Stuart with another man if he'd died that day. It was a reasonable concern for an eleven-year-old, and I wondered whether my children would ever question my decision to date less than a year after their father's death.

Even Stuart, my stalwart pal, had trouble reconciling his support with his discomfort. In any social gathering, Stuart was always the comic relief, the gentle rascal who made you blush, but also had your back. September 11 subdued him. His struggle to contain his own grieving to comfort others weighed heavily, and maintaining a light manner became an understandably precarious endeavor. Stuart took me aside during the party to share that I "needed to know" he was having a hard time "fully accepting" my dating Derek. I knew Stuart really liked Derek, but was surprised how shaken he was to see him with Doug's kids in this family setting. He was probably reflecting on his daughter's concerns, but it was still jarring to hear my dear friend's painful admission. His honest comments—maybe too honest—made me realize that I needed my friends to check their unfiltered concerns and simply support the façade of normalcy I was trying to uphold. I was struggling enough to accept Derek's increasing role in my life; it didn't help to hear my own anxieties articulated.

16

Without the usual pressures of biological clocks or the L- or M-words, one might think my relationship with Derek remained, on the surface, a "friendship with benefits" that never delved deeper than our favorite foods and what movie tickets to buy. On the contrary, our connection became surprisingly more intimate since neither of us focused on the future. Derek and I didn't dance around who called whom, who initiated plans, whether we were spending too much or too little time together. For the first time in my dating career, I was seeing someone who welcomed unvarnished conversations, which were more revealing than most men were willing to endure in the early stages of a relationship. I think our circumstances required that kind of openness. Instead of making me feel my loss was something I needed to manage on my own, Derek encouraged me to tell him stories about Doug, to help him get to know the husband and father whom we'd lost. We asked each other blunt questions and neither of us shied from frank answers. Once I asked him whether my already having children might be a hindrance. He deadpanned, "The children aren't the problem. You, on the other hand, could be."

The more we saw each other, the harder it was to contain our feelings. The parameters we'd set—no future talk, no deep analysis, no labels—kept getting blurred. By late winter, we saw each other nearly every day. Even Michael started to notice. One afternoon after school, he told me over a bowl of popcorn, "Mommy, you go out to dinner with Derek more than anyone else."

Busted. He'd called me out. I could no longer pretend Derek was just a private vacation from my life. He'd already taken Michael to a Knicks/SuperSonics game at Madison Square Garden and applauded Julia's ballet recital from a front-row seat. Derek seemed to delight in their antics in a way that told me he wasn't just being polite. I found myself asking his advice on discipline and debating whether *Days of Thunder* was a proper movie for him to watch with Michael on a Sunday afternoon (we decided it was not). Occasionally, Derek and I would spend a winter weekend alone in the Hamptons while my parents stayed with the kids in the city. (I'd invited Derek to store his car at my house to avoid Manhattan garage fees.) And vials of insulin had found a home in my medicine cabinet in the city. Since the day we met, he'd talked about how urgently he wanted to buy a loft in SoHo or the Village, but six months later he still lived with two strangers on Amsterdam in his ramshackle bedroom with the milk crate TV stand. Whom were we kidding?

Our struggle to maintain some semblance of independence raised the awkward question *How would we handle sleepovers?* Yes, Derek had started sleeping at my apartment. I fretted about it, but it seemed better than hiring a live-in sitter so that Mommy

could stay overnight at her paramour's house. Besides, did anyone really expect me to swear off sex for the rest of my life at the
age of thirty-six? Was there some kind of widow's code of ethics
that required us to shake hands in the lobby and say good-night?
It wasn't 1955, and I wasn't living at the Barbizon Hotel. Still, I
didn't want the kids to wake up to find a shirtless man brushing
his teeth in Howard's second sink in Mommy's bathroom. Derek
and I worked out a plan worthy of James Bond. He would come
over after the kids were asleep and leave by 5:00 a.m. before they
woke. On weekends, he'd return with bagels and croissants as if
he were popping by to have breakfast. Michael and Julia were
thankfully unaware, which allowed me to feel less tawdry and
even a little responsible.

Frankly, Derek's overnight stays were a little confusing to me.
We weren't married, yet I'd grown accustomed to his coming
over after a night out. Sometimes I didn't react well when he
decided not to stay. One Friday night after a movie, Derek told
me he wanted to spend the night at home, and I went off the
rails.

"Why? It's Friday. You don't have to do anything tomorrow,
do you?" I asked incredulously, since I'd already mapped out the
evening in my mind.

"No, I don't have anything scheduled. I just want to spend a
night at home." Derek saw my face and looked puzzled. "What's
the big deal, Jen? Can't I stay at my place once in a while? I've
hardly been there in days."

"Whatever." I turned a cold shoulder. "You don't have to
walk me home." We were standing on Broadway and West Sixty-
Seventh Street, about the midpoint between his and my building. I turned on my heel and waved good-bye without looking at
him. Fuming the entire way home, I couldn't understand why I

was so agitated. By the time I got to my elevator, my heart rate slowed, and I finally hit on the answer. *I wasn't his wife.* I called Derek the second I walked into the apartment.

"Hello?"

"I shouldn't have given you such a hard time about not coming over tonight."

"What the hell was all that about?"

Shit, I was in trouble. "Well, I think I may have confused you for my husband. I know we're just dating, not married, but I think I sometimes conflate the two. I am still so accustomed to going home every night with my husband that, when you refused, I wasn't prepared. Going out with you feels very much like going out on date nights with Doug. It shouldn't, but the physical process feels the same. I'm so sorry for my little tantrum. I still don't have a handle on things yet."

Derek laughed that gentle, soothing laugh I was growing to love. "I'm glad you called. I wasn't sure what to make of your foot stomping."

"I hope you can be a little patient while I learn to date like a normal person."

"I don't want a normal person," he answered directly. "I'll talk to you tomorrow."

· · · · ·

One Sunday morning while I was sharing silver-dollar pancakes with Michael and Julia at the Elite Café on Columbus Avenue, Michael suddenly announced that he wanted me to find them another father. I finally understood that "spit takes" don't just happen on sitcoms.

"What?" I sputtered. "You really want a new father?"

"Yes," my son answered with a serious expression. "I want a stepfather."

I was flabbergasted. Where were they hearing about stepfathers? "I know you miss Daddy. I do, too. Do you really want me to find someone else?"

Julia started nodding her head vigorously. She was just four years old and wanted to be a part of the conversation. "Mommy, I want a daddy, too."

Ouch. I was hoping not to have to have this conversation for a long time. But they were perceptive children. They knew something—someone—was missing. Every day they had to hear classmates talk about their daddies and watch kids on the street being swooped into sturdy arms on the way to the playground. No child wanted to be different.

"Okay, if you guys really want Mommy to try to find a stepfather, you have to understand that means Mommy will have to date. Do you know what dating is?"

Michael and Julia looked at me blankly. How was I going to explain dating? "When a person dates, she is giving someone chances to see if her family will like him. That means Mommy will have to go out to dinner a lot with that person to decide whether he is someone we should like."

"Like Derek," Michael piped up.

"Yes, like Derek, smart guy," I said, holding his sticky face in my hand. "Right now we're giving Derek chances to see if we like him. Is that okay with you guys?"

"I like Derek," Julia said through a mouthful of pancakes.

"I'm glad you do," I said. "But you two don't need to worry about this. Mommy will decide first if the person we're 'giving chances to' is someone she thinks is special. If he is, I will let you know, and then you can decide if you like him."

"What if we don't like him?" Always the practical one, Michael zeroed in on the doomsday scenario.

"Honey, if you don't like the guy, he's outta here!" Michael giggled as I imitated a crazy umpire throwing a guy out at first base. "I would never give you anyone you didn't like. You and Julia always come first. I love you guys—we're in this together as a team. Are you with me?"

I raised my milk shake and clicked the plastic cups lifted by Julia and Michael to seal the deal.

Months after that Sunday breakfast, Derek and I met for dinner on a wintry Saturday evening. My parents were visiting, so no covert sleepover that night. When Derek walked me to my building, he leaned down for a kiss good-bye on the snowy sidewalk. I rubbed his ears against the cold with my gloved hands and touched my forehead to his. "Thanks for dinner, Derek."

"It was fun. See you later. Love you."

"Me, too. Bye."

I turned to go inside, and stopped at the elevator. What did he just say? It must've been a reflexive endearment, not the big L– declaration. He didn't mean *I love you* as in *I'm in love with you*. We made a deal—no falling in love, no major commitments. And anyway, I didn't love him. Except, I did. No matter how I tried to rationalize—we're just companions, he's a diversion, we're just keeping it light—I couldn't deny how real my feelings were. We were falling in love, and it was getting ridiculous and burdensome to pretend we weren't.

Soon after, Derek and I were eating takeout sushi in my kitchen when he asked whether he might spend the summer weekends at my house in East Hampton instead of renting a share house with his buddies.

"You're comfortable with the idea of staying with the kids and me every weekend?"

"Of course I am. I'm pretty much doing that now, only the kids don't know it. What do you think?"

I thought how exceptional he was to trade a summer of fun with his single friends to take Julia to the bagel store on Sunday mornings. Despite our agreement to keep things day-to-day, Derek was already planning our summer together. But moving in with us would make our relationship public. Factual. We'd be a real couple. Did I really want that?

"I would love for you to spend the summer with us," I told him hesitantly. I was in a box. It would be so easy to have him to ourselves, but wouldn't it be unfair to allow Michael and Julia to get attached to him only to get hurt again if he and I separated? If they were to wake up to find Derek at the breakfast table, I needed the kind of commitment we'd promised not to ask of each other. I needed to know he was looking at a future with us—yet, at the same time, the thought of that terrified me.

Derek gave me a funny look. "What are you thinking? I can tell something's up because you're biting your lower lip. You look just like your daughter when she's trying to hide something."

"You know me too well, and I'm not sure I like that. Of course I want you to spend the summer with us, but it would be a big step. If we're going to do this, I need to know what it means."

"What do you think it means?"

I suddenly had a courage I'm sure I lacked before 9/11 redefined me. "You have to know I wouldn't even think about inviting you to the Hamptons if I didn't love you." I said it—the word just hovered.

"I love you, too," Derek said gently. "Of course I love you. Do you really think we've been casually dating for the last seven months?"

I couldn't determine whether I was ecstatic or despondent. How could I love someone else? "I guess it was impossible to casually date someone like me. I never intended to fall in love with you, but you've been such an unexpected gift. And I'll be honest: these feelings hurt as much as they make me happy."

"Honey"—he called me that by then—"let's just see where things go and not try to force anything. If we're ever going to have a future together, we need to take the risk and allow our relationship to develop in the open. I promise you, I'm serious about us. I love you, I love the kids, and I want us to be together."

I was gobsmacked. These were words I never thought I'd hear again, let alone wait for. But there I was—looking over tins of tuna sashimi at the man who was making me believe for the first time that second chapters weren't just movie conceits.

The next day, I called Lynn, my therapist, and scheduled an extra session. I'd been struck by a sudden conviction that I was doing a terrible thing. Sex wasn't a betrayal; falling in love was. How could I abandon Doug? Sitting in Lynn's office, I was once again curled on her chair picking at my cuticles.

"What happened?" she asked.

"Derek and I said, 'I love you.'" I started to cry. "My stomach hurts, and I feel like I'm cheating on Doug. How can that be? I've been seeing Derek for months, and only now I feel I'm betraying my husband?"

"Slow down, Jennifer. Let's talk about this." Lynn handed me the tissue box. "I think what you're feeling is what you've been saying all along. A physical relationship with Derek works because it doesn't touch the part of you that loved Doug. But, as you two get closer, you're having a harder time denying that it may be possible to feel deeply for someone else."

"How can I possibly love someone else?" I was crying hard. "I still love Doug. I miss him every day. I can't be happy without him. I thought I could just go through the motions and paste a smile on my face. But I can't actually *be* happy, can I? Not when Doug is missing everything. It's not right." I sank deeper into the chair.

Lynn leaned toward me and said calmly, "You haven't yet integrated Doug's loss. Until you do that, you're going to have a difficult time moving on."

"I don't want to move on!" I was yelling now. "I have no intention of integrating anything. Can't I just live in the gap between loving Doug and dating Derek?"

"Yes, for a while. But eventually you're going to have to reconcile that you're living without Doug. You're functioning, laughing, planning, and, yes, loving someone else. You won't leave him behind if you fall in love with Derek. You'll carry him with you, but you have to come to terms with finding happiness without him."

I couldn't accept what she was saying. I missed Doug so much at that moment. "Can't I just be Doug's wife and create a separate other person who is pretending to live a full life?"

"Jennifer, you are both of those people. I know you hate when I say this, but give it time."

17

"What would you think if I invited my family to come to New York for Thanksgiving?" Derek posed this loaded question as we walked Michael and Julia around the Central Park Zoo in late September, following the second anniversary of the attacks. In many ways, the second anniversary was harder than the first. My therapist told me that the first year was about survival, the second about learning to live. She promised I'd start to feel more "normal" by the second anniversary. During our session on September 10, I told her she had twenty-four hours to make good on that promise.

Still, I had to admit that, for the most part, my life was settling into a routine I'd venture to call manageable. Even happier. Derek and I were solidly a couple now. We'd spent a restful summer in the Hamptons, and the kids were thrilled to have Derek all to themselves. Every Thursday evening we would pile into the car to pick up Derek at the East Hampton train station. The kids would wait restlessly with the other children on the platform in their flip-flops and plastic sunglasses, watching for signs of the coming train. When Derek finally emerged from one of the cars carrying his briefcase in one hand and a gym bag in the other, Michael and Julia raced to hug him first.

Derek was basically an overgrown adolescent, a rule-breaker, full of mischief. The kids couldn't get enough of him. Whether he was getting chased by Julia with a hose while washing the cars or letting Michael do cannonballs into the pool from his shoulders, Derek was a whirlwind of juvenile high jinks that reduced my kids to hysterics. Belly laughs were a sound that had been absent for too long from our home, and I tried to celebrate my children's joy without lingering on what was missing. Even Derek and I were finding ways to stretch our time together. Instead of driving back to the city in Sunday-afternoon traffic, he began to extend his stay until Monday mornings, when he would catch the early train or the occasional seaplane dressed in one of the suits he stored in my house. By the end of the summer, Derek had appropriated a bedroom closet and a spot in the garage to store bicycle tires, a dozen water bottles, and an extra-long triathlon wet suit.

When the second anniversary arrived, I asked Derek to come with me to Cantor's memorial service. It was reassuring to have him there—to understand what it felt like to have so many family members under one tent. He held my hand through the service and hugged me protectively when I burst into tears as Doug's name was read by the surviving partners. He greeted the Gardners with familiar warmth and received high fives from LaChanze's daughters. A wife of one of Doug's late partners remarked how brave and composed Derek was to accompany me to the service. I agreed. This was not an easy room for anyone, especially a new boyfriend. But Derek's particularly gentle confidence eased the strangeness, and his being there felt more hopeful than jarring.

That said, it was surreal for me to find myself thanking a widow for complimenting my boyfriend at our husbands' memorial service.

"So, what do you think? Can I invite my family to come for Thanksgiving weekend?" The kids were busy watching the polar bear, Gus, swim desultory laps around the toy-strewn pool of his pen. "No one in my family has ever been to New York. The long weekend would be a perfect time to show them around."

"It's a great idea. Who would come?"

"Everyone: my parents, sister, brother, his wife, my two nieces, and my nephew. I want them to get to know you. And Michael and Julia will love the 'cousins,' Samantha, Sevren, and Kate—they're all about the same age."

"I would love to meet your family. Let's do it. But, you know that my parents and Doug's parents will be at Thanksgiving dinner, too."

"I think it's time we bring everyone together."

I wasn't expecting that. Derek had always been a singular entity for me, a blank slate who fell from the heavens and landed on my foot, unattached and available. When friends asked about his background, I'd joke how lucky I was that Derek was never married, had no kids, and the in-laws lived three thousand miles away. But, I'd wondered if we would ever get to the point where we'd want to connect our families. This is what typical boyfriends and girlfriends did when a relationship got serious. But I'd bet most first meetings with a boyfriend's parents didn't include two children and the girlfriend's deceased husband's parents. I made a mental note to refill my Xanax prescription.

Thanksgiving had always been Doug's and my favorite holiday. Living on the second floor of a Central Park West apartment building gave us prime seats to watch the annual Macy's Thanksgiving Day Parade pass below. Every Thanksgiving morning, Doug and I would set out a spread of coffee and bagels to greet the steady stream of friends and their children who'd spill into our living room to enjoy the floats and balloons. When the parade ended and our last guests shuffled out the door with their bundled children in tow, my mother commandeered the kitchen to prepare the turkey with her famous stuffing with the shaved carrots and mushrooms, the source of many years of tussles between me and my sister for the last spoonful. Doug and my dad retired to the couch while I'd quickly get the apartment ready for dinner with our parents and sisters in the late afternoon.

But, after 9/11, Thanksgiving ceased. Doug's family escaped to their place in Boca Raton, and my children and I retreated to the Hamptons for the lonely weekend. Hosting Derek's family would bring life back to Thanksgiving, but I worried how it would feel to re-create our traditions for a new family.

When I told my parents and the Gardners that Derek's family would join us for the holiday, their immediate reaction was positive. They liked Derek, but he was still a cipher to them. Meeting his family would give him context. Joe Gardner assured me he wanted to meet Derek's family, that it was "important" to make them feel welcome. My parents were understandably protective and even a little tentative. They knew Derek was a good person, but they still looked for confirmation that his intentions were genuine. Transporting his entire family across the country for the holidays was an encouraging indication that he was committed. Still, my mother confessed she started to feel uneasy as the day approached. She was thrilled that I'd found love again, but worried the day would be too emotional for her. It had only been two years, and suddenly we were welcoming a new family at Doug's table. I felt similarly unsteady. I still lived in two parallel worlds where I was Doug's wife in one and Derek's girlfriend in the other.

It turned out we didn't need to worry. Derek's family arrived en masse Thanksgiving morning in a whirlwind of colorful scarves and light hair. They all had tall, rugged builds, delicate noses, blue eyes, and alabaster skin. Derek looked identical to his father, Steven, minus the gray hair and wider build. His mother, Kristine, was shorter with brown hair and a cackling laugh that charmed me immediately. David, Derek's brother, and his wife, Jennifer, introduced Michael and Julia to their three towheaded children. Immediately, the five of them darted to the living room, where Michael showed the Trulson kids where the best seats were to watch the parade. Derek's thirty-year-old sister, Amy, embraced her brother and rolled her eyes when he asked her how much of a hassle it was to get everyone organized that morning.

The Trulsons' unbridled enthusiasm was infectious and soon everyone relaxed. Kristine immediately engaged my animal-lover daughter in a discussion about her two cats, Timmy and Lily. Michael challenged Samantha, Derek's oldest niece, to bedroom basketball. Steven and my father wandered around the apartment talking about skiing, old cars, and sightseeing. Derek was beaming; he looked so proud watching his family interact with mine. I think he wanted to show his parents that his decision to move to New York was the right one. His mother confided in me that she worried about Derek living so far from home, but was grateful I was looking after him.

If the Trulsons were shocked that Derek picked a widow with two children as his girlfriend, they didn't show it. Amy told me what really surprised her was that Derek actually wanted all of them to meet us. She claimed Derek hardly ever introduced women to his family, so an airlift to Manhattan was a monumental event. Even David said he was excited because they never thought Derek would settle down. All things a Jewish mother would want to hear about her daughter's boyfriend—I'd remember to share those comments with my mother later.

The Gardners arrived in the afternoon, and I couldn't have been more impressed (and relieved) with how effortlessly they mixed with the Trulsons. Steven and Joe had similar career backgrounds as real estate entrepreneurs, and the two were soon exchanging war stories over Scotches. Charlotte, Kristine, and my mother huddled in the kitchen, sharing gardening tips and helping prepare the meal as the familiar Thanksgiving smells wafted from the oven throughout the apartment. Derek played bartender and at one point chastised me for not having gin when I knew we'd be hosting his WASP family. I come from Jewish teetotalers; we were more likely to have an extensive supply of rugelach than a properly stocked bar.

My father performed his favorite magic tricks for the kids in the playroom. By the end of the performance, Zadie had three new fans so taken with him that they named their new hamster Zadie a few weeks later. I was so happy to see my children playing with the Trulson children and the adults mixing so seamlessly. But at times I felt weary from the smiling and the chitchat; I noted a heaviness hovering over this Norman Rockwell portrait. On a few occasions, I retreated to the bedroom to catch my breath and throw cold water on my face. *I miss you, Douglas. You're not forgotten.* My mother later admitted she was doing the same thing in the guest bathroom. A few cathartic tears got us through the day.

The dining room table sparkled with candlelight from the crystal votives Doug and I received as wedding gifts. Most of the china and silverware were from our wedding, but I tried to focus on who was in the room—the gathering of West Coast and East Coast at one festive table. The children were comfortably ensconced in the adjacent foyer at a long, plastic card table covered with a waterproof tablecloth and decorated with paper turkeys, autumn leaves, and orange napkins. When we all sat down, for a brief moment I think everyone simultaneously felt Doug's absence. Joe immediately redirected our attention by raising his glass to toast the Trulsons, welcoming them to New York and thanking Derek and me for bringing everyone together. Derek followed with a hearty "To in-laws," which brought a round of laughter and set a light tone for the gregarious holiday dinner that followed.

When everyone had finally gone home and the dishes were done, my parents took Michael and Julia for their baths. Derek and I sat at the kitchen table picking at my mom's chocolate-chip cake to do the postgame analysis on the evening.

"Do you think your family had a good time?" I asked.

"Are you kidding? I don't even know where to begin." He extolled my parents "shuttle diplomacy" between Doug's and his family and affirmed that Zadie was a huge hit with his nieces and nephew.

"Your family is wonderful," I told him and meant it. "It was so nice to have that energy in the house again."

"It's hard to believe our parents are from two totally different worlds, but seem to be the same people. It's like my mom and dad traveled across the country to meet their neighbors."

I laughed. "I know. How funny was it when your dad and mine walked over to the New York Historical Society to see the Alexander Hamilton exhibit? I think they talked about American history minutiae the entire afternoon."

"Exactly. They both tell the same meandering stories with

too many details. Was your mom nervous about what to expect from my parents? My mother certainly was. I think she was afraid she'd look like a country bumpkin in the big city."

"Please, that's silly. The moms could've talked about gardening and grandchildren for days." I noticed Derek's buoyancy. He looked like a proud father. "You look happy."

"I am. It was so important for my family to see what my life was like in New York. They only know Manhattan from movies and *Sex and the City*. They needed to see that the people here aren't the stereotype, all slick, rude, materialistic strivers—"

"Not that there's anything wrong with that," I interjected, gesturing at the two of us.

Derek smirked. "I wanted them to meet you and the kids so they would understand why I'm never going back to Seattle. Having my parents here makes everything real. This is my home now."

"Do they think it's strange that you picked a widow with two children?"

"I think my parents are just thrilled that I chose an adult. They're already in love with Michael and Julia—two new grandchildren would be icing on the cake."

"So, the verdict is success?"

"It was perfect. Except for one thing, my little Jewish friend. Next time, remember the gin."

18

After Thanksgiving went so well, the next logical move was for us to go to Seattle for Christmas. For my Jewish family, Christmas Day represented the best Vermont ski day of the year, when the slopes cleared and a page over the loudspeaker for "Dr. Shapiro" set off a mad dash to the base lodge by dozens of people. Later, when I moved to New York, my Christmas routine with Doug became a daylong movie marathon followed by the obligatory Chinese takeout dinner. Now I was cautiously anticipating Christmas sweaters, eggnog, and Secret Santa gift exchanges. Derek couldn't wait to introduce Michael and Julia to the joys of tearing into a pile of presents on Christmas morning. For the first time in my life I had a two-page Christmas gift list.

Derek and I took the kids on a shopping spree in Times Square, where we ransacked a souvenir shop for taxicab banks, New York Knicks caps, stuffed animals wearing I ♥ NY T-shirts, and other Gotham-branded tchotchkes that Derek's nieces and nephew and young cousins might enjoy. Over several weeks, I carefully selected presents for his family and the names assigned to Derek for the annual cousin gift-exchange. Derek, meanwhile, continued to bring home a ridiculous amount of swag for Michael and Julia, which left me shaking my head. "It's too much, Derek. They don't need all of that."

He would not be deterred. "You don't get it, my love. That's the whole point of Christmas with the Trulsons. It isn't about need. It's about celebrating. Just roll with it, honey, the kids are going to *love* Christmas in Seattle. Now, where are the FedEx boxes? We have to ship all of this stuff to my parents."

Since our first date, Derek and I always enjoyed bantering about our cultural differences. Tongue firmly planted in cheek, we regularly poked fun at each other's stereotypical WASP and Jewish behaviors, such as his affection for pink and yellow ties and my inability to hold my liquor. It was our private language—our way of adjusting to each other's background. I'd given Derek Doug's copy of *The Complete Idiot's Guide to Understanding Judaism*, which he read over a few days. Through the years, Derek has participated in and embraced every Jewish life-cycle event—from brises to bar mitzvahs to funerals. He even gave an enthusiastic delivery in English of an aliyah (the prayer before the reading of the Torah) at Michael's bar mitzvah service. My friends often comment that Derek is "good for the Jews," and Derek savors his role as what he calls a "goodwill ambassador."

Similarly, I appreciated the culture in which he was raised, even though he and his family weren't at all religious. I grew up in a largely non-Jewish hometown, and I think Derek would agree that I knew more about the history of Christianity than anyone in his family. I had the occasional pang that Derek didn't share my heritage, but it wasn't a stumbling block for us. I was always going to be a Jewish mother raising Jewish children. If Derek had been religious and wanted us to adopt the more spiritual aspects of his faith, I'm not sure our relationship would have worked. But Derek wasn't interested in that. He never considered changing the way I raised the kids; he just wanted to participate and share with them some of the family traditions he'd loved since childhood. Christmas in Seattle would give the kids and me a more intimate connection with Derek and shed valuable light on how he was raised.

The moment we crossed the threshold into Derek's boyhood home, I knew I wasn't in Manhattan anymore. Kristine took Christmas decorating seriously; her house was a showplace of holiday cheer. From the colorful lights to the welcome mats, every corner was festooned with Christmas bric-a-brac. Silver reindeer candlesticks were set on the dining room table, and red and green Santa hand towels decorated the guest bathroom. On top of a breakfront, Kristine arranged an eclectic gathering of old-fashioned Christmas-caroling figurines; each meticulously costumed doll represented a member of the Trulson family. A large sleigh was set atop a bookshelf, with a sparkling eight-foot tree in the sunken living room. I don't think I'd ever seen such an elaborately decorated tree, with each gold and silver ornament, ribbon, and garland carefully placed to balance each branch. Next to the tree sat a vintage jukebox playing a medley of Frank Sinatra and Bing Crosby Christmas tunes. My children could barely contain their excitement when they discovered the mountain of presents around the tree.

Within minutes of our arrival, Steven gleefully hustled Michael to the basement to show him the basketball hoop he'd installed in anticipation of our visit. Kristine presented Julia with three new personalized Christmas stockings she'd made for us. They were stuffed and hanging on the mantel next to the rest of the family's. I got a pleasant shiver when I noticed photographs of Michael and Julia from Thanksgiving thumbtacked to Kristine's bulletin board in the kitchen alongside her family pictures. *Our children are on someone's wall in Bothell, Washington. Doug, can you see this?* At the various Christmas parties held over several days, all of the aunts, uncles, and cousins showered my children with the same attention they did their own. It was as if Michael and Julia had always been a part of their clan. Neither Doug nor I came from a large, effusive family; it was astonishing to be accepted without reservation.

Still, the cultural differences between the Trulsons and my little family were stark, but mostly entertaining. At the Christmas Eve family gathering attended by more cousins than I could count, I was introduced to Kristine's elderly mother, who identified strongly with her Icelandic roots. She was a tough old bird, as Derek described her, and suffered from the early stages of Alzheimer's. At one point she motioned to me and said, "I understand you're Jewish."

"Yes, that's true," I replied hesitantly, while Derek and a few of his cousins snapped to attention.

She studied my face for a few seconds and pronounced, "Yes, but you're obviously not practicing."

I know one might hear prejudice in her comments, but from where I was standing, she was more curious than wary. I actually think she was expecting me to have my head covered and be wearing the more modest dress of an Orthodox Jew. I assured her that my children and I were definitely Jewish, but we were excited to be a part of the Trulson holiday celebration. Derek and his cousins chuckled when I turned to them and whispered out of her earshot, "Besides, I've gotten pretty good at this Jewish thing over the years. I don't really need to 'practice' anymore."

Derek's family certainly knew how to throw a Christmas party. Trays of personalized Santa mugs were passed through the room filled with fish chowder (apparently a Trulson tradition) that one of the aunts always prepared. Derek's cousins were boisterous, growing more so with each spiked eggnog and gin and tonic downed throughout the evening. I could barely keep up with everyone's names and family connections, but it didn't matter. Like an amoeba surrounding a food source, the Trulsons absorbed the kids and me into their revelry until it became impossible to tell where they ended and we began.

When it came time to hold the cousin gift exchange, Derek's family had it down to a precise ritual. First the children gathered in a vibrating scrum of nervous anticipation until Derek's cousin Andrew appeared wearing the Santa hat. He then called each child's name, one by one, to retrieve a proffered gift. No one opened a present without first finding the giver and thanking him or her with a hug and kiss. I was concerned Michael and Julia might feel left out when the other children opened their piles of gifts; I'd only provided a few small ones since we'd already exchanged the bigger presents at Chanukah. But my worries were misplaced: every aunt, uncle, and cousin deluged my children in holiday loot. They were working overtime to show Derek how easily they'd welcome his New York "family." I was oddly at ease in this room of joyous strangers. Indeed, it was hard not to laugh watching Michael and Julia scramble for their gifts and turn to the crowd to shout, "Who's Aunt Laurie?" before the frantic sprint over ottomans to deliver the required peck on the cheek. Within minutes, the kids were covered in torn wrapping paper, and Derek delightedly shouted across the room, "See, I told you, Jen, they're ours now."

The adult gift exchange was equally rambunctious. Gardening gloves, Carhartt pants, cookbooks, and Jean Naté bath splash were opened amid a chorus of oohs and aahs. I knew I was far from home when one of the cousins passed large boxes to each adult in the room and asked us to open them at the same time. In unison we reached into our gifts and pulled out identical sea-shell-encrusted macramé wind chimes. Derek chortled in my ear, "How many Upper West Siders do you know who have one of these? You're going to be the envy of all your friends."

Unlike the several days of parties leading up to the main event, Christmas morning at Derek's parents' house was a more relaxed, quiet affair with just the siblings and Derek's nieces and nephew. We arrived at nine from the Washington Athletic Club where we were staying and positioned the kids on the white couch in the living room to wait for the go-ahead to tear into the presents. Steven donned the Santa hat, and for the next two hours the room was a blur of flying ribbons, torn paper, and muti-lated plastic containers of Barbies, Nintendo games, and football jerseys. Michael and Julia joined the frenzy like two veterans—soon they and the "cousins" were hanging over the back of the couch, beseeching Steven for their turn like baby birds squawk-ing to be fed. I sat on Derek's lap as we monitored the activity from a large, upholstered chair.

Derek wrapped his arms around me. "How are you feeling? It's surreal that you're here, right?"

I was just thinking how crazy it was that I was spending Christ-mas morning in a Washington living room. I was supposed to be with Doug watching a movie at the Angelika and finalizing plans for our annual New Year's Eve party, not sticking paper bows on my sweater in the Pacific Northwest. Just as the lump started to form in my throat, I looked at Michael and Julia with their candy canes and new Washington Huskies T-shirts squealing as they reached for yet another gift from Santa Steven. They were ecstatic with the kind of unmitigated euphoria children who haven't lived through the sudden death of a parent normally experience on such an occasion. My kids weren't thinking about where they should have been—they were fully present where they were, surrounded by grandparents, cousins, aunts, and uncles who lived for moments like this. Derek looked so proud of them, as any husband or father would be. Maybe we did belong here, and I should just breathe and let the moment be. (Our place in the Trulson clan was indeed cemented the following year, when Kristine presented Julia, Michael, and me with our own Christmas-caroler figurines to join the family's collection on the breakfront. My heart nearly burst when I saw the Michael doll holding a small, plastic basketball that Kristine had glued onto his tiny songbook.)

Eventually, the tidal wave of presents subsided to puddles of wrapping paper and discarded blister packs. The adults were hungry, and we dragged ourselves over to the dining room table where Kristine had set out a buffet. Up until that time, I thought I'd done admirably for a Jewish girl navigating three days of rowdy Christmas parties and traditions. That is, until I saw the "buffet"—a small platter of red Chinese pork with a bowl of French's yellow mustard, a crock pot of cocktail wieners drowned in a thick, spicy brown sauce, two plates of carrot and celery sticks, and a bowl of defrosted frozen shrimp with cocktail sauce. My jaw unhinged. This was the spread for the *entire* day? I know I had no right to judge, but I was a Jewish mother who generally stored three days of leftovers after a midday snack. This spread barely sufficed as appetizer; it certainly was not my idea of a full day's menu for twelve people and the drop-ins who spontaneously appeared every few hours.

Obviously I couldn't say anything, but throughout the long

day I tiptoed into Kristine's kitchen to ransack the cupboards. As my children rationed Cheerios, and I withered from starvation, I finally grabbed Derek and pushed him into a quiet corner.

"How can your family possibly get through this never-ending day with no food?"

He looked at me as if I'd lost my mind. "Honey, we're gentiles. We're drunk by ten. We don't notice."

By the next holiday season, I made sure we were prepared. I shipped a Zabar's basket filled with bagels, spreads, and good pastrami to his parents, timed to our arrival, and Derek, my hero, found the only food kiosk in Pike Place Market open on Christmas morning. It was a Chinese dumpling purveyor. Jewish Christmas in Seattle was born.

·····

In the late spring of 2004, I called Derek at his office from my kitchen in East Hampton. A huge moving truck had pulled into the driveway to deliver the motorcycle Derek told me he'd built in Seattle. Since I was ignorant of throttles and baffles, I expected an oversize moped. Instead, the men unloaded a chrome and black-leather monstrosity I later learned was a Harley-Davidson Road King. If it had wings, it could have been a Cessna. In a box that arrived with the bike I found well-worn leather riding jackets, steel-toed boots, and a brimless black helmet that looked like something Colonel Klink would wear. I couldn't believe this behemoth was going to sit in my pristine garage with the Chevrolet and Julia's Barbie princess bicycle. As I watched the scene unfold, I told Derek over the phone, "Oh my God, you're definitely not Jewish, are you?" Derek reassured me I'd love the bike, which I did, mainly at a safe distance from my front stoop. The

motorcycle was only the beginning. Derek's passion for the auto-
motive arts was deeply ingrained from a lifetime of afternoons
building and restoring 1960s muscle cars with his father in their
workshop. Today, Derek is often glued to the computer searching
eBay for elusive parts or rummaging for original Shelby manuals
in a stranger's musty attic. Next to his side of the bed lie what I
affectionately refer to as Derek's "car porn"—an archaeological
trove of car-industry magazines, such as *Hemmings Motor News*,
Car and Driver, the National Corvette Restorers Society news-
letter, and *Hot Rod,* stacked in teetering piles. A few years ago I
finally acquiesced and agreed to let Derek expand the Hampton's
garage to accommodate his "hobby." My gardening tools and pool
toys were replaced by a hydraulic lift, metal workbenches, and a
heated concrete floor. His garage was nicer than our living room.
My poor car's new home was under a tarp on the side of the
house. Most summers you'll find rusty exhausts, carburetors, and
other unidentifiable car parts strewn about the driveway with a
shirtless Derek smeared with grease under the hood of his latest
project. Often his trusty assistant, Julia, is standing there handing him tools and helping with tire changes—and I must admit,
I rather enjoy the view.

19

"I'm engaged!" Erin Richards, my good friend and partner in grieving crowed into the phone. When I received her ebullient call that Jon had proposed, I admit I was rattled. It wasn't that I didn't support their relationship; on the contrary, I was ecstatic that my friend had found someone who adored her and her precious son, Asher. Jon Frankel was a documentary filmmaker and the national correspondent for CBS's *The Early Show*. Like Derek, he was an athletic, strikingly handsome bachelor, who'd nearly exhausted the local dating pool when his life turned on a dime the moment he glimpsed Erin leaving a movie theater and fell in love with the young, widowed mother. Unlike us, Erin and Jon were ready to marry less than a year after first meeting each other. What unsettled me was that her news made me question my own relationship. Was something wrong with me that I couldn't imagine marrying Derek? And what a hypocrite I was, clinging to the illusion that I was still Doug's wife while Derek's dress shirts hung in my closet.

Derek and I flew to Aspen to attend the late-afternoon ceremony on a crisp September day in 2003. It was held in the open air as the sun started to set with the guests sitting in a circle of chairs around the bride and groom. Derek and I sat next to Doug's confidant Stephen Merkel, Cantor Fitzgerald's general counsel, and his wife, Robin, whose sympathetic ear I frequently bent in the several months following the attacks.

Erin looked delicately beautiful in an ethereal white dress, with her long brown hair loosely falling around her lovely face. Jon couldn't stop the tears as he greeted his bride and Asher, now his son, under the rustic chuppah of branches and Aspen leaves. The deeply emotional service tenderly honored Erin's late husband, Greg, and celebrated the couple's determination to rebuild. It was impossible not to be overcome when Jon's brother delivered his poignant, beautifully articulated tribute to Erin's courage and Jon's commitment to be a father to Asher. People cry at weddings, but not like this. Everyone dissolved in a puddle of tears. After the loss and sorrow of the past two years, we all yearned for the happy ending that finally seemed possible.

I didn't anticipate how difficult it would be to watch the rabbi wrap Jon, Erin, and Asher in a tallith, the ceremonial prayer shawl, as he blessed their new union. I wanted to get carried away like every guest around me. It was an exquisitely hopeful moment. But the image of swaddling a family under a magical scarf to symbolically protect them was too much. It seemed too tidy, a made-for-television ending. How could a wedding make everything okay? I buried my face in Stephen's shoulder and gripped Derek's hand. I definitely wasn't ready to be someone else's wife. Huddled between Derek and the Merkels, I was obviously still caught between my past and present, unable to decide where I belonged.

Still, Erin and Jon's ceremony became a turning point for me. I felt the unrestrained joy of their brave step into a hopeful future. Of course, their marriage didn't erase the past or tie up every loose end. Erin's loss was still grievous, indelible. But their marriage gave us all a glimpse of a second wind, a reason to celebrate that was well earned. She was visibly happy in a way none of us ever thought we'd be again. Erin and Jon gracefully proved that it was possible to stand in two worlds—the old life and the next—and be true to both.

.....

There wasn't one definitive moment when Derek and I decided to get married. As he grew more attached to Michael and Julia, and we continued to spend as much family time together as we did alone, marriage became a *fait accompli*. Derek abandoned his quixotic search for a SoHo loft and remained in his cheap apartment with rotating roommates. I only had to suffer the morning walk of shame past my doorman once to realize I was too old to be dating like a college freshman. Managing Derek's clothes and mail at two different addresses became unwieldy. Neither of us wanted to play "house" anymore; Michael and Julia deserved a real family. After a trip to Disney World, where Derek rode the Small World ride in the Magic Kingdom, posed with Goofy, and cut Julia's pancakes at the Chef Mickey breakfast, it was impossible to deny that he was becoming a father.

Until February 2004, I was still working my way through the administrative nightmare of the federal Victim Compensation Fund. It was to be my last act as Doug's wife—to petition the federal government to "compensate" me for the murder of my husband. How odd it was to refresh my legal training to make the case for personal devastation. It was a ghastly task I felt I had to complete before I could contemplate moving forward with Derek.

My application filled two thick volumes of legal briefs and affidavits documenting the impact of Doug's loss on our family. Included were psychiatrist reports, graphs of Doug's income projections, Michael's drawings, and family photographs. Our entire life as husband and wife reduced to the equivalent of two phone books. Everything about the process was demeaning, especially when I had to plead my case over speakerphone to Special Master Ken Feinberg. For all I knew, he was playing Brick Breaker on his BlackBerry while I tearfully recounted the agonizing moment I first told Michael and Julia their daddy was never coming home. When Mr. Feinberg abruptly interrupted to inform me that my "children are lucky" because they were so young they "won't be damaged," I nearly threw the phone through my attorney's glass conference-room door.

With that ordeal behind me, I started to imagine marrying Derek. He'd already proven to be the kind of father Michael and Julia deserved. I'd seen him dab his eyes the day Michael hit his first basket in an organized basketball game. He joined me for the kids' parent-teacher conferences in the fall and hooted from the sidelines when four-year-old Julia suddenly stopped counting dandelions and started to dribble the soccer ball purposefully toward the goal. I once asked whether he wanted to have children of his own. I was thirty-seven years old; if we were going to have more kids, we'd need to do it quickly. Derek told me he'd love to have a baby, but not enough to allow a biological clock to set the pace for us. "I need to know we're good as a couple first," he told me. "It's more important than rushing things so we can have a baby." Though I was relieved to hear that, I worried he'd one day be disappointed if we never had a child together. His answer surprised me.

"To be honest, I don't have the kind of ego that demands I have my 'own' child. The way I see it, I already have two. Michael and Julia are mine. They're all I could ever want."

What is it about widows? One could argue that men can't help falling for the mythical damsel-in-distress. But I think Derek was more attracted to my independence; I didn't need his wallet, status or DNA. He asked me once what I wanted from him. "The real thing," I answered. I missed being loved, more than I wanted to admit. But I didn't want Derek unless he knew unequivocally he couldn't imagine his life without us. Doug wouldn't want anything less for his family.

·····

"Quick, let's get downstairs before it gets too dark outside." Halloween 2004 had arrived, and we were once again hustling Michael and Julia out the door to trick-or-treat. Michael bounded into the foyer in a bedraggled skeleton costume, while Julia meowed in her pink-and-white kitty-cat getup. We'd just returned that afternoon from a weekend in Boston to attend a bat mitzvah. We paraded the kids with their pumpkin bags past the doorman to join the throngs on Sixty-Eighth Street, which always held the annual closed-street festival.

What a difference a few years made. As I snapped pictures, Derek confidently steered Michael and Julia through the lines of revelers. He looked like every other hapless father schlepping the kids' spare jackets and begging his daughter not to dart ahead of the pack to the next candy basket. "Can we go home now?" he pleaded wearily when we finished two laps of the street.

The kids raced us up the back stairs, through the kitchen door, and into the playroom, where we immediately sprawled on the yellow carpet to mine the kids' treasures. Michael had been given a homework assignment from his second-grade teacher to create a bar graph measuring the number of each type of candy he collected. I helped him segregate the Kit Kats from the Starbursts, while Derek inhaled the Swedish Fish from Julia's collection. Suddenly Julia exclaimed, "Look what I got!" In her hand was a black box, opened to reveal a clear, square stone on a simple white metal band. Inexplicably, I thought it was a toy.

"How nice, Monkey. Someone gave you a ring. It's beautiful." I turned back to Michael to continue to sort his candy. Derek started to chuckle. I heard him say under his breath, "You've got to be kidding," and looked up to see him roll onto his back laughing even harder. Michael clambered over to him, and soon the two were giggling and pointing at me.

"What's so funny?" I demanded testily.

Derek sat up and replied deadpan, "Look again, genius."

Julia handed the box to me. The second I felt the soft velvet, I realized what an idiot I was. Derek had hidden an engagement ring in Julia's candy bag. I couldn't breathe. "Oh my God," I whispered. "Is this real?"

Michael clapped, Julia looked puzzled, and Derek leaned over to where I was sitting on my knees, holding the open box in both hands. "Yes, honey, of course it's real. I love you. Will you marry me and make us a family?"

I looked at my sweet Derek with his arms wrapped around Michael and Julia. "Of course I will. I can't believe it. I love you."

Derek turned to the kids. "Is it all right with you that I marry your mom?"

"Yes!" the kids yelled in unison. We all dove on top of Derek and rolled around the carpet in a tangle of arms, legs, kisses, and tears.

Michael was excited. He proudly told me Derek recently asked him for permission to marry us during one of their Sunday-morning walks to Starbucks. Julia was happy, but a little confused that I'd "stolen" her ring. Derek kissed me gently as we disengaged from the family embrace to allow the kids to finish sorting their candy. He took the ring out of the box and slipped it on my finger. "Kids, we're now officially a family."

Instantly I felt a bolt of panic.

"Derek, how am I going to tell the Gardners?"

"Don't worry," he reassured me with a smile. "I already did."

I couldn't believe what I was hearing. "What do you mean you 'already did'?"

Derek wrapped his arms around me. "Remember, a few weeks ago, when I was late for Michael's baseball league meeting?"

"Yes."

"I went to visit Doug's parents at their apartment after work. Over drinks, I asked Joe and Charlotte for their blessing. They deserved to be the first to know. I wanted to assure them that I would take care of you and their grandchildren. They also needed to know I would always protect Doug's place as Michael and Julia's father. Jennifer, they were so gracious, and I think Joe really enjoyed being asked. I promise, they both reacted positively and wished us happiness."

I was floored. "I can't believe you did that. I didn't think I could possibly love you any more than I do right now. You're a . . . miracle. If there's a universe at work somewhere, I think Doug would be very proud of you."

The Gardners did indeed cheer our news, as did my parents, who were overjoyed to welcome Derek into the family. My first call after notifying the relatives was to Allison and Howard. They were present the night Derek stepped on my foot in the Hamptons; it was fitting that they'd be the first to hear of our engagement. Within an hour, they appeared at our door with a cold bottle of Dom Pérignon, and we toasted to happy marriages and our enduring friendship.

In the ensuing months, Joe and Derek developed a real camaraderie. It was good for them to spend time together. They were kindred spirits in the real estate world, and Joe often invited Derek to tour a building or have lunch to regale him with stories of his early days in the business. At one lunch, an acquaintance of Joe's approached their table to say hello. Derek told me Joe introduced him as his "son-in-law." Noting the surprise on Derek's face, Joe shrugged with a smile and said, "Eh, it works. I like it."

20

"We're going to be bridesmaids, right? There's no way you're not having us as bridesmaids."

Pam, Vicky, and I were sitting in the bay window of Pam's house the day after Derek's proposal. I was wearing my new ring with a wad of Scotch tape stylishly wrapped around the band to keep it from falling off my finger.

"Seriously, Jen, who are you going to ask to be bridesmaids?" Pam asked.

"You're not going to make me wear an ugly dress," cautioned Vicky.

I smiled. They were really grilling me, rapid-fire.

Pam continued to press. "You're obviously going to have your sister as matron of honor, but you're not going to have just family, right? We're going to be there, too. And Allison."

"We get to pick our own dresses. You're not making us wear awful matching dresses?"

"Oh my God, we're too old for that, right?"

"Okay, enough already," I interjected to stop the hilarious barrage. "I've barely had a second to process the proposal. I haven't even thought about a wedding party."

"What do you mean? You're not going to have bridesmaids?" Pam's pretty face fell.

"I didn't say I'm not having them—"

"But you look like you're unsure. You look hesitant."

"Clearly I'm having them, now that you've given me so much time to think about it," I chuckled, patting Pam's arm. "Vicky, I hope you like orange taffeta."

What a nice feeling it was to sit between my two dear friends joking about a happy occasion for a change. We were actually giggling and gabby. My friends had sacrificed so much to take care of me the last three years; I knew I wanted this wedding to be as much a thank-you to them as it would be a celebration for my new family. As Vicky wrote in an e-mail I kept, "While nothing eradicates the past, your marriage signifies that good fortune eventually finds the brave. It is an end to the bitter and the beginning of the sweet." And none of it would have been possible without them.

Cards, bottles of champagne, and bouquets arrived at our door for the next several weeks. I fielded buoyant phone calls and e-mails from Derek's Seattle friends and family. It dawned on me that Michael, Julia, and I suddenly had new aunts, uncles, cousins, and grandparents. I couldn't help but laugh at the thought of our tiny Jewish family being absorbed by Derek's hardy crew. With the Gardners in New York and my parents a train ride away, we were surrounded by family.

It was definitely a happy time, but Derek and I knew that a ring didn't magically clean the slate. Like all newly engaged couples, we had to learn how to mesh our independent lives without killing each other. When I married Doug, I was a twenty-eight-year-old attorney, living in my first cramped apartment in New York. He and I were at the beginning of our lives, ready to build a family. Now I was a thirty-eight-year-old mother of two with an established life, juggling basketball practice, school conferences, and the family finances. I didn't quite fit the traditional definition of "bride" and wasn't completely sure I'd be able to release my autonomy over family decision-making.

My fear of losing control came to a head when Derek suggested that I consider selling the apartment. Of course, it was a reasonable request—how could we live together as a new family in Doug's apartment among all of the ghosts and memories that still haunted the place? I didn't want Derek to feel he'd moved into "my" life. We needed to make a fresh start in a new home. But I was feeling the strain of having to uproot once again. My entire life was a series of starting-over moments: Longmeadow, Boston, Manhattan—single woman, wife, mother, widow, girlfriend, fiancée. I just wanted our marriage to signal a resting place. Exhausted from grieving, I wanted the happy ending already.

A new home wasn't the problem; it was Derek's seemingly cavalier resolve to jettison the old one. To him, selling the apartment was a prudent family decision and real estate transaction, but for me, it was much more. Though I agreed to put the house on the market, I wasn't prepared for how quickly we'd sell it and sign our names to a purchase agreement for a new condominium on the Upper East Side. I suddenly felt Derek was trying to bulldoze my past, which wasn't accurate, but that's how I felt nevertheless. Worse, I discovered he had deeply entrenched ideas concerning renovation and décor. Where Doug deferred to my taste and design choices, Derek had an opinion on everything from doorjambs to throw pillows. He'd spent his life building houses, and our marital home became his master project. I felt I'd been relegated to observer, my decorating ideas and storage suggestions taken under advisement. Where Doug might ignore my input but do it in a playful way, Derek just said, "Trust me. I know what I'm doing." I'd lost control, which didn't sit well with me.

Derek didn't consciously intend to marginalize my efforts or opinions. He was just genuinely excited to build our new home. Nearly every day for weeks, he'd scratch layouts for me on a piece of paper, tear pictures out of shelter magazines, and gleefully describe how happy we'd be in our new surroundings. For the first time, he had an official role in our household and wanted me to recognize his good intentions for our family. Instead of embracing his enthusiasm and trusting his judgment, I balked. I couldn't help myself. His confidence scared me, and I couldn't see past what I thought he was asking me to leave behind. I got tense and contrary when he showed me changes to the floor plans. Where he wanted pedestal sinks in the bathrooms, I argued for cabinets. When he suggested an open kitchen and family room, I insisted on walls to separate the spaces. We had our first real fight over the size of a linen closet. Neither of us had great skills in the art of compromise even under the best circumstances, but Derek was confused by my sudden lack of trust. I needed to relearn how to be someone's partner and have faith that this man whom I loved would take care of us.

. . . . .

A strange bliss washed over me the first time Derek left for work the morning after he officially moved in. I opened all of his dresser drawers and smiled at the neat rows of socks and T-shirts. I wasn't snooping (really); it was just so nice to see a man's clothes in the closet again. Yes, his extensive bicycle gear was spilling out of the kids' toy closet, and protein shakes and PowerBars threatened to become the only staples in the kitchen, but I didn't care. These things weren't relics of a former life, the heartbreaking reminders of a man who wasn't coming home. Instead they were harbingers of a normal future—Derek lived here and we were a family restored. Could I have done without the dirty socks left on the floor three inches from the hamper? Possibly, but it reminded me of Doug and made me laugh. But did Derek also have to leave the bathroom as if a tsunami had rumbled through? I wish someone could explain to me how a man is able to drench a ceiling from just a shower and a shave.

It was challenging to combine lives when both of us were fully formed adults with well-honed idiosyncrasies and personality traits. We had to work harder to find common ground than I did with Doug. He was a more natural fit, and we were much younger at the start of our adult lives when we first met. Derek and I, however, were from two completely different worlds. He was a bachelor whose life revolved solely around his interests and needs, while my life centered on two small children and the trauma of their father's death. During an argument, Derek proclaimed that I'd have to get used to his ways since he'd been a single guy for so long. I countered in a fit of pique that I didn't have time to train him; we were a moving train and he'd have to jump aboard. Clearly, we both needed to learn how to relinquish the reins to give us a chance to build the life together that we knew we were fortunate to have.

Derek's parents instilled in their children traditional values of independence and self-sufficiency. Chores, table manners, and family dinner were requirements in the Trulson household. Though they spent a lot of time together after school and on vacations, playing sports and working on cars, I suspect demonstrative expressions of physical affection were rare. Derek subscribed to the stiff-upper-lip philosophy: unless you were hemorrhaging, you carried on without complaint.

In contrast, my family hugged, coddled, overprotected. Sure, my sister and I learned manners, responsibility, and self-reliance, but nearly every whine, kvetch, or skinned knee elicited an empathetic squeeze or McDonald's sundae. We certainly didn't get everything we asked for, but Jayme and I were indulged by a "hands-on" mom and dad who stroked our hair, kissed the boo-boos, and showered us with praise and a few too many unsolicited opinions.

Derek's and my diametrically opposed perspectives came into sharp focus the moment he saw me kneeling in front of eight-year-old Michael, tying his basketball sneakers before a game.

"Jen, honestly, why on earth do you continue to tie his shoes when he is perfectly capable of doing it himself?"

"Because, my dear, one day his wife won't let me."

Sometimes Derek's independence morphed into detachment. The kids and I often joke that it's "Derek's world," and we just live in it. Whether he's researching a new gadget, working in the garage, or surfing eBay for parts, Derek can disappear for hours. He becomes entranced with his task, the radio silence broken only by the occasional snack run. I can't count the number of times we've been late for dinner reservations because of what I call Derek's "failure to dismount." On more than one occasion, he's endured my scolding to get off the apparatus because it was time to go. Besides getting lost in his hobbies, Derek often gets lost on a sidewalk. I could be in the middle of a sentence, and suddenly Derek will have vanished. A bright color in a store window or the sudden urge to get ice cream distracts him, and he's gone without a word. Once Derek disappeared into the Times Square subway station during the Christmas shopping rush, leaving me abandoned at the teeming entrance to fumble with my wallet in search of a MetroCard. At first, his seemingly ungallant behavior infuriated me. I was accustomed to a man who held doors and helped me over snowdrifts. I wanted Derek to protect me, to take care of the little things, such as killing water bugs in the bathroom or walking three paces slower when I'm wearing stilettos.

But I knew it was stupid to compare—Derek was not supposed to be Doug. I was no longer a young single girl just starting out in a new city. Maybe I didn't need the same things I once thought I required. Weathering a tragedy, running a household, and raising two children on my own proved that I didn't need anyone to hold me up. I'd become more hard-driving, rigid, and focused. These traits had helped me survive, but they had to be softened if I was ever going to rebuild our family with Derek. At times I was so concerned with what Derek wasn't doing, I missed the things he *was* doing. He never treated me as if I were damaged. He challenged me to be more spontaneous, less cynical, and showed me that I didn't need a rescuer, but an equal who'd allow me to release my death grip on the control stick. I also knew he'd never wanted anything in his life more than he wanted us. Derek could be taught to help me out of a taxi, but his devotion to us and can-do outlook outweighed any lapses in manners. So what if he sometimes talks on his cell phone while I pull the suitcases off the baggage carousel at the airport? I'll be sure he makes it up to me the next time there's an 8:00 a.m. soccer carpool on a cold Sunday morning.

······

When Derek officially moved in, Michael and Julia were thrilled by their new family and delighted in greeting Derek at the door every night when he came home from work. The parallels weren't lost on me, but nothing could dim my joy at seeing Michael and Julia wrestle Derek to the ground before he had a chance to change clothes. They needed a father, and whatever discomfort I experienced over Derek's stepping in for Doug, I needed to quash it for the kids' benefit. Derek was a gift, and Michael and Julia couldn't get enough of him.

The question of how to label Derek's relationship with the kids became a challenge. We didn't want Derek to be the "stepfather" because, for me, that implied divorce and diminished Derek's full-time parental role. But he certainly wasn't their father. The kids called him D, a nickname they coined the first summer Derek stayed with us in the Hamptons. Derek's friends from Seattle used *DT* as a casual moniker, but I think the kids adopted *D* as a way to make him theirs. I liked the way it sounded; more intimate than *Derek*, but not quite *Daddy*. My children and I have had a lot of D's: Doug, Derek, Daddy. Often it became an exercise in oral gymnastics to identify Derek properly. I cannot count the number of times I've called him Doug. Thank goodness he answers to both and, amazingly, has never corrected me.

The morning after Derek's proposal, Julia climbed into our bed to snuggle before school. After chastising me for still wearing "her" ring, she turned to Derek and said, "Good morning, Daddy." Derek's eyes popped and cheeks reddened. "Well, good morning, Daughter," he said, pulling her into his arms for a hug. Derek looked at me over the top of Julia's head and mouthed, "Did you hear that?" I nodded, too overcome to speak. Our engagement had given her two parents, and Julia was ready to test-drive her new father the first minute she could.

Putting a name on Michael's new status with Derek was complicated. Michael continued to call him D, and we simply followed his lead. It didn't matter what Michael called him; what mattered was cementing their bond. I didn't think Michael cared that Julia called Derek "Daddy," until the day he came home distressed from a wintry afternoon of sledding in Central Park. Derek and Howard had taken the kids to enjoy the fresh snow at a hill near the Great Lawn. Sitting on his bed with the door closed, Michael tearfully confided to me that Julia kept yelling, "Daddy, pull my sled!" and "Daddy, ride with me!" in front of the Lutnicks.

"She just kept calling him Daddy the whole time. You have to tell her to call him D."

I think hearing Julia holler "Daddy" in front of Howard resurrected Michael's angst. He panicked that Derek would replace Doug and worried Howard would think we'd forgotten Daddy. My heart ached that my little boy once again had to wrestle with these issues, but I had to tread lightly since Julia's need to identify Derek as her father had to be respected.

"Michael, it was hard for you to hear that today, wasn't it?"

"I didn't like it. Why does she have to call him Daddy?"

"Well, you know Julia doesn't remember Daddy, right? You and I remember him, but she was too young when he died. She only knows Daddy from the stories we've told her and the pictures she's seen. Honey, for Julia, the word *daddy* has always meant a hole, an emptiness, something others had that she didn't. Did you know that every time Julia used to hear another child or parent say 'Daddy,' she'd whip her head around to see who it was? Once she even asked me not to take her to a birthday party because she was worried daddies would be there."

Michael looked at me wide-eyed and asked, "Did she really turn her head when she heard people say 'Daddy'?"

"Yes, my love. Can you see that, with Derek, Julia finally gets to have what her friends have? She calls him Daddy because he fills the hole and loves her the way she always dreamed a father would love his daughter. I don't want us to make her think her feelings are wrong, do you?"

Michael shook his head.

"You should know," I continued, "that I understand that for you, the word *daddy* isn't just a word. For you and me, Daddy was a person who we love and miss so much. Derek is *not* Daddy and would never, ever try to replace him. He loves you more than you can imagine and respects your memories. He just wants you to be comfortable. You don't ever have to call him Daddy or Dad. But I need you to know that, even if one day you did call him that, no one would ever think you didn't remember your father. Howard knows you remember him. Your friends know it, too. Everyone knows Daddy existed, and you don't ever have to worry that people will forget him."

Michael was quiet for a moment. I could tell he was processing my words and trying to empathize with his sister. I saw the relief on his face when he was able to recognize Julia's needs were different from his. I couldn't stop kissing his ruddy cheeks when he told me, "It's okay, Mommy. Julia can call him Daddy. She needs it."

I think our conversation was a crossroads for Michael. Until then he was still wrestling with his loss, trying to be loyal to Doug while accepting Derek as a substitute father. Knowing that labels and a new marriage didn't expunge the past helped free Michael to deepen his rapport with Derek without guilt or reticence. I didn't even realize how much Michael actually felt for Derek until his second-grade teacher gave the students an assignment to write an essay about someone they considered a hero. The year before, Michael wrote about Doug for a similar assignment, but this time, he told me he wanted to write about D because "D helped us smile again." He wrote:

> *My hero is Derek, who I call "D." He came into our life when we really needed him. He makes Mommy feel good which makes our whole family feel good. I also think he is a hero because he has a great relationship to me. He comes to my games, helps me with my manners and every weekend he takes me to Starbucks for donuts. I know he is going to be a good dad. Most important, he is good at sports, which I like.*

We kept his essay a secret from Derek until Michael delivered it as his toast at our wedding reception several months later. A typed copy still hangs on the wall in our office.

21

The alarm chirped at 6:15 a.m. I jerked awake in the pitch-dark room, and for a few seconds I had no idea where I was. "Good morning, my bride," a sleepy Derek murmured into my ear as he spooned me. We were waking up in a luxurious suite at the New York Palace Hotel. It was May 14, 2005, the morning of our wedding. Michael and Julia were with Nana and Zadie at our apartment, and Derek and I decided to take advantage of the hotel room. I know it was sacrilege for the bride and groom to spend the wedding eve together, but with two kids walking down the aisle, we were hardly the blushing bride and nervous groom. It had been a long and arduous journey to get to that morning; neither of us was going to miss one glorious second of it.

We'd decided to have a traditional wedding. It took some time for me to acquiesce to the pomp. I'd already walked down the aisle in a ballroom with white-rose centerpieces, crystal chandeliers, and a string quartet playing Pachelbel's Canon in D. I felt like a bride then; now, I was more interested in just getting on with the business of being married. But I realized that Derek was a first-time groom. His family and the entire Seattle posse would fly to New York to witness their boy say "I do"—not just to me, but to the kids and to his new life in New York. I don't think many of his friends and family ever thought they'd see the day that Derek, the perpetual bachelor and free spirit, would get married. That in itself warranted a first-class celebration.

Most important, Derek and I felt that Michael and Julia deserved a real commemoration. Second weddings often are low-key affairs with just close family and perhaps a few friends in attendance. We certainly wanted to have a dignified ceremony that honored Doug's memory as well as our newly reconstituted family, but neither of us wanted the kids to get the mistaken impression that our wedding was something to be concealed or downplayed. We all needed to be surrounded by our friends to show the kids that everyone we loved supported them. Indeed, our stalwart friends who stood by us through the dark aftermath of the attacks, and every year until this improbable day, definitely deserved a raucous celebration. Our wedding would be a chance for them to exhale.

Still, I couldn't quite wrap my head around the "bride" concept. Somewhere in the mix of kids' birthday parties, basketball practice, and supervising homework, I found myself on the sixth floor of Bloomingdale's with a price gun in my hand perusing wine goblets. I'd gamely fought the idea of registering for housewares; I already had an apartment filled with cutlery, dishes, and napkin rings. But, after the tenth person berated me for being a bridal Scrooge, I succumbed and inundated my poor fiancé with e-mail attachments filled with photographs of place settings, candlesticks, and bath towels.

Truth be told, I did enjoy many aspects of planning the wedding. Unlike the first time, when two sets of parents opined on everything from flowers to menus, now I was—in the immortal words of George W. Bush—the decider. And I decided that our wedding would have a modern, New York style—we wanted to treat Seattle to Manhattan at its most chic. Happily, Derek readily agreed and became an eager partner in the planning. I now had a man who loved to shop, and his attention to detail was unparalleled. He once spent nearly twenty minutes in a store comparing the fabric of one blue shirt with a nearly identical one. I gently snapped him out of his reverie by reminding him we were in Banana Republic, and he should just buy both so we could move along. Suddenly I was the one looking for a newspaper and a chair while my boyfriend interminably perused the racks for the perfect ensemble. It wasn't lost on me that Derek didn't need me the way Doug did to coordinate his wardrobe, but having a modern dandy for a fiancé had some advantages. He knew the difference between a stacked and a stiletto heel, practiced impeccable grooming, and when he commented on an outfit I was wearing, I unequivocally trusted his opinion. He took daring fashion risks (white patent leather belt, anyone?), but sometimes his sartorial choices broke through the envelope he was trying to push, such as the absurd linen cargo pants printed with large pineapples that he insisted on wearing to a very public fund-raiser. I had to laugh, and besides, he was so handsome he nearly pulled it off.

Wedding-gown shopping, however, was the bane. One would think that after years of exploring New York's retail jungle, I would relish the hunt for the perfect dress. But this task did me in. A white dress on a thirty-eight-year-old mother of two? I was supposed to do white only once, but as they say, if you want to make God laugh, tell Him your plans.

I made an appointment at the stately Vera Wang boutique on Madison Avenue and astutely schlepped Pamela with me to try on gowns. At the top of a sweeping spiral staircase, a cool, beige-carpeted jewel box of an atelier filled with white, ivory, and pink confections awaited us. The young sales associate introduced herself: "Hi, my name is Alicia. Which one of you is the bride?" When I sheepishly raised my hand like a seventh grader getting caught talking in class, Alicia turned to me and said with a big, toothy smile and an effusive shrug of her shoulders, "Congratulations! It's so exciting."

Ugh, I hated when salesclerks gushed. I know an engagement is a communal moment when a woman is allowed to bask glee-fully in the goodwill of strangers, but I felt too jaded for all of that froth. Pam and I exchanged knowing looks, pasted on our own toothy smiles, and followed Alicia to view the racks of satin and lace hanging delicately on plush hangers.

"So, Jennifer, do you have any ideas about the style of dress you'd like to wear on your big day?"

Would a black sequined gown strike the wrong note? "Something sophisticated, elegant, and decidedly unbridey" was my reflexive response. "No poufy skirts, bustles, corsets, or lace-covered bod-ices. It's my second wedding. No meringue."

"Oh, um, that's no problem," the flustered Alicia replied, her eyelids fluttering but her professional smile frozen in place. "We have many styles for you to see."

Pam and I flew through the racks and within minutes pulled several possible choices. I entered the dressing room with the gowns, and Pam waited for me on a beige couch near the three-way mirror. When I had on the first dress, I walked out to the mirror to assess the situation. Standing next to me was a young blond girl in her twenties with her elegantly coiffed, equally blond mother. They seemed the epitome of Upper East Side breeding. The petite girl was wearing a sugary, strapless confection with a voluminous skirt and sweeping train. I was in an ivory, backless sheath with spaghetti straps. My eyes met Pam's in the mirror and we nearly doubled over in laughter. The virgin and the cougar. Yes, indeed, God certainly has a sense of humor.

Derek and I decided that we would have a Jewish wedding ceremony, complete with a chuppah and the traditional breaking of the glass. In deference to Derek's lack of religious conviction, I promised we'd make the ceremony "Jewish-lite" and forgo the traditional Hebrew vows in favor of personal ones written by us. We'd also asked seven friends to read poems or original compositions instead of the traditional Sheva Brachot, the Seven Blessings usually recited at a Jewish marriage ceremony.

We wanted a rabbi to perform the ceremony. I knew one from several of the Jewish organizations with which I'd worked over the years. Rabbi Sharon Davidson also knew Doug and me as a couple and stirringly presided over his memorial service. She'd gotten to know Derek through social events and watched him grow from my charming date to Michael and Julia's adored father. I knew she would be able to weave sensitively our family's tender past with our expectant future and couldn't imagine anyone else blessing our marriage. I worried, however, that she might balk at marrying an interfaith couple. She agreed to meet Derek and me at her office to discuss the wedding.

"I normally wouldn't agree to do this, but after 9/11 I'm starting to rethink my position." Sharon leaned forward over her desk, while Derek and I shifted on hard chairs like two applicants seeking approval for a loan. "Jennifer, you've been through so much, and Derek has been there for you and the kids from nearly the beginning. You're about as Jewish as they come and committed to raising your kids accordingly. You, Derek, have already gotten quite the initiation into Jewish life, moving from Seattle to New York and joining forces with that one. I see you as someone who will support her and respect that aspect of your family's life."

"I love the Jews. I'm a big fan," my helpful fiancé declared. "But I don't see myself converting. You don't need me to be on the team, do you?"

Sharon laughed. "No, you don't have to convert. But believe me, I'd be thrilled to help make that happen if you change your mind. Honestly, I do think you actually might be 'good for the Jews.' Did you know that, during different periods of the Diaspora when Jews were expelled from their homes, there were gentiles who'd move with them? They'd help pave the way for the Jews to establish communities in new lands. Those gentiles were ambassadors. Derek, in a sense, you're one of them. You're paving the way for Jennifer, Michael, and Julia to find and rebuild a new home after losing theirs. I would be honored to marry the two of you."

·····

With the question of clergy settled, I started to think about how to include Doug in the service. Of course, our wedding was about us and the kids, but we wanted to honor him and his indelible place in our family. We knew our ceremony would be emotional, especially for the New York contingent, who lived through the nightmare and still mourned. But, we certainly didn't want to turn our wedding into a maudlin tearfest. We needed to balance our acknowledgment of the past with our celebration of a happy future.

We decided that I would walk down the aisle alone after Michael and Julia joined Derek at the chuppah. It seemed wrong to ask my father to give me away again when he'd already done that once before. I guess Doug was going to have to give me away this time. Some believe Doug threw Derek into my path that night at Saracen. If that were true, then he might as well walk me down the aisle.

I asked Julia one night while I was giving her a bath how she thought we should honor Daddy at the wedding. She told me she wanted all of us to light a candle the way we always did for him on September 11. Jews traditionally light a *yahrzeit* candle on the anniversary of a person's death and attend synagogue to hear his or her name read to the congregation. I thought Julia had a beautiful idea, but instead of a simple candle, I suggested that she and I make a woven one with five separate wicks representing each member of our family to light at the ceremony. Julia assigned each of us our colors, and I found a candlemaking company on the Internet from which to order waxes and several lengths of wicks. After an afternoon of rolling the crumbly wax sheets, Julia and I proudly constructed a lumpy multihued candle—Michael, Julia, Derek, Doug, and I all entwined in a child's rainbow of colors.

·····

"Are you going to go for a run now?" I called to Derek while he checked his blood sugar in the black-and-white marble bathroom of our bridal suite.

"Definitely. I'm going to go home, change, and do the loop around Central Park. I'll probably stop by the Boathouse to see how things are going."

We'd picked the Central Park Loeb Boathouse for our ceremony and reception. We didn't want a staid hotel affair, and the Seattle contingent deserved a real taste of New York. What could be better than getting married at a historic restaurant in Central Park on a warm spring evening, overlooking a lake dotted with ducks and swans and rowboats?

The night before, we'd held our rehearsal dinner in a private dining room at the Soho Grand, a trendy boutique hotel on West Broadway known for its sexy cocktail lounge. Our intimate dinner eventually spilled into the lounge, where we invited all of Derek's Seattle guests to join us to continue the party. Derek's buddies mixed easily with his New York boys, especially since many of them had recently attended Derek's far-flung bachelor weekend in Reykjavik, Iceland. Leave it to Derek to forgo Vegas for a frozen island near the arctic circle. I'm still relieved they all came home in one piece.

I was about to turn on the television to check on the weather when Derek came out of the bathroom and sat on the side of the bed. We just looked at each other in silence for a while until Derek started to snicker.

I sat up. "What is it?"

"I don't know. I was just thinking how much my life has changed in such a short time. We're getting married in a few hours. How *crazy* is that?"

"Insane. And wonderful. And surreal. You're happy, right?"

Derek scooped me into his arms. "So happy, honey. We are so fortunate; I've never wanted anything more in my entire life."

It was difficult to leave this plush cocoon, but it was time to start the day. I planned to stay at the hotel, work out at the gym, and wait for the hair and makeup people to arrive. My parents and Julia would come in a few hours to get dressed with me. Allison,

Pam, and Vicky would also join us later for the limousine ride to the Boathouse. Derek would keep Michael with him at the apartment to join the ushers, who would gather there to get ready.

"Good-bye, babe," I said as Derek headed for the door. "Next time you see me, I'll be the one in white."

"Don't worry. I'll find you."

·····

My parents arrived with Julia at 11:30. The tears started at 11:31. We had a half hour until makeup—so much emotion, so little time. Julia handed me her ivory garment bag holding the pink flower-girl dress with matching ballet slippers she'd chosen from a treasure trove of frothy dresses at Magic Windows. "Can we get dressed yet?" she asked, clearly anxious to move on from the sniffling.

"Soon, baby," I said, squeezing her tightly. "We have to get our hair done first. Will you show me how you're going to walk down the aisle?"

Julia giggled and sprang from my arms to demonstrate. She and her brother had been practicing all week to their song, Van Morrison's "Warm Love." No violins this time around. No Bach or Vivaldi. A custom-mix CD of our favorite songs would serenade this wedding party down the aisle.

The hairstylist arrived at noon and started to work on Julia's wispy locks while I took a shower. Karen, Allison's friend who was at Saracen the night I met Derek, walked through the door bearing enormous cosmetic cases. She was an accomplished makeup artist who did my makeup on my wedding day ten years before. It felt reassuring to have her with us.

Finally, it was time to get dressed. The photographers had arrived and were snapping pictures of everything from our shoes to the dresses to a silly portrait of me in curlers. After my hair and face were complete, I helped Julia into her layers of pink tulle and tied the satin bow at her back. She looked angelic, with a few strands of her delicate hair swept into sparkly rhinestone barrettes over her right ear. "My baby," I exclaimed when she twirled for the cameras. "You are the most beautiful girl I've ever seen. I need to squeeze you right now." I knelt down, and Julia threw her arms around my neck. "Daddy is going to fall over when he sees you, Monkey."

"I love you, Mommy."

"I love you, my daughter."

"My tights are itchy."

"Of course they are."

I looked up in time to see Jayme make a frazzled entrance after having her hair and makeup done at an Upper East Side salon. "Help me," she begged. "I *hate* my face!" Karen quickly ushered her to a chair and commenced triage. Vicky, Pam, and Allison, who'd arrived earlier, were sitting at the dining table talking to my mother, who had changed into her fuchsia gown with an elegant portrait neckline. Her blue eyes and clear skin were highlighted strikingly by the deep color of her dress. Pam was wearing a romantic "Pammy pink," strapless gown with her hair swept back prettily. Vicky, glamorous in her stunning silver-sequined sheath and chandelier earrings, chatted with Allison, who, at five months pregnant with her fourth child, looked positively sybaritic in a gold, draped gown. My girls rocked.

When Jayme's face was sufficiently beautiful again, she quickly changed into her dusty-rose dress and joined me in the bedroom to get me into my ensemble. After too many visits to bridal salons and boutiques, I'd finally settled on a sleeveless white silk-charmeuse gown with a deep-*V* décolleté neckline. A white silk flower was sewn strategically at the base of the neck-line, and the back of the dress swept the floor. This hot number was a far cry from the voluminous, off-the-shoulder ball gown of silk shantung and lace that I wore when I married Doug. But today was ten years later, and I wasn't that girl anymore. I put Derek's engagement ring on my right ring finger and attached a glittery pair of diamond earrings I'd borrowed from a friendly jeweler. Here comes the bride. Again.

·····

After a champagne toast and a few more pictures, we piled into two black limousines for the short drive from midtown to the entrance to the Boathouse at Seventy-Second Street and Fifth Avenue. It was a crystal clear afternoon, and Central Park was teeming with people of all ages enjoying the late-spring air. We drove into the parking lot, and among the joggers, fussy toddlers in strollers, and motley street performers, I stepped out of the car in my gleaming white dress. A few passersby stopped to take a peek, but this being New York, a wedding party in Central Park hardly caused a ripple. Our intrepid wedding planner, Robyn Karp, motioned for us to follow her through the side door, and we entered the Boathouse.

"Are you ready to see where it's all going to happen?" Robyn asked as she stood in front of the silk douppioni curtains that obscured the ceremony area from the rest of the reception room. Around me band members were readying their instruments, and Robyn's staff was busily setting the tables, while the florist put finishing touches on the Lucite boxes of white peonies we'd cho-sen months before as centerpieces.

"Let's do it." Robyn pulled open the curtains, and I melted.

I couldn't believe how magnificent the room looked. The lush chuppah featured two enormous bowers of cascading white tulips and green cymbidium orchids. Tiny glass balls holding votive candles twinkled from their wired perches throughout the verdant structure. Robyn had set the chuppah in front of the large bay windows overlooking the lake, the late-afternoon sunlight dramatically illuminating the profusion of flowers and filtering over the simple podium beneath. Rows of white chairs filled the room, and Julia's homemade taper rose from its holder on a light green tablecloth under the chuppah next to my silver kiddush cup and laminated copies of our vows.

"Don't screw up your mascara," Jayme admonished, while Allison, Pam, and Vicky tried to stop me from crying.

"You're getting farklempt," Allison yelped comically like Mike Myers on *Saturday Night Live.* "Talk amongst yourselves."

"Do you love it?" Robyn asked. "I can't get over the chuppah."

"Robyn, it's beyond anything I ever imagined. I don't understand. I know we picked the flowers and designed everything, but I never expected the canopy to be that lavish on our budget."

Robyn took my hand. "Stephen went overboard. Your story touched him, and he wanted you to have an unforgettable day. You should see the bathroom. You can barely see the sink through all of the hydrangeas."

I looked around the room. Maxine, Jayme's eighteen-month-old daughter, cruised along the rows of chairs while Scott snapped pictures of her. My parents hugged Derek's mom, who'd just arrived with Derek's sister, Amy, and sister-in-law, Jennifer. The cousins Samantha and Kate made a beeline for Julia, who was still twirling in front of her reflection in the bright windows. Amy and Jayme joined my bridesmaids and me under the chuppah for pictures. Just as the photographer told us to smile, Derek and his ushers poured through the curtain. "Oh, no, there she goes," Pam and Vicky cried simultaneously as I disintegrated once again.

Derek stood quietly at the top of the aisle, resplendent in an ivory dinner jacket and champagne-hued bow tie among his black-tuxedoed wedding party. He was radiant, but what caused the new flood was the little boy smiling under Derek's protective arm. Michael was dressed in an identical ivory jacket and tie. Derek's mini-me. Man and child. Father and son. It was too much, yet it was exactly right. Michael was going to be okay. We were going to be okay. I just needed to stop the waterworks.

"Oh, honey, you look great." Derek swept me in his arms, while my parents swarmed their grandson.

"You look quite debonair yourself."

"Did you see Michael? I gelled his hair like mine."

"I saw. The two of you are tearing my heart open. He looks so good next to you."

Derek's eyes watered. "He's beautiful, and I'm emotional. During my run this morning, I was bawling by the first mile. It was ridiculous, I couldn't stop. I swung by here and chatted with Robyn while she and her crew were setting up. I think it finally hit me what it meant to be a husband and a father. I thought about how much you and the kids have gone through and how lucky I am to be here with you. I love you, honey. We're going to have a great life together, I promise."

The next hour raced by in a flurry of family photographs and bride and groom portraits on the long deck overlooking the water. Julia, Kate, and Samantha danced on the steps leading to the lake, while Michael and Sevren looked on, pulling at their stiff collars and pretending to throw each other into the water. My dad and Steven walked around arm in arm declaring themselves "the grandfathers" to anyone within earshot. From the far end of the deck, I watched the two families playfully mingle and couldn't help but note the improbability of how we all came together.

"I know what you're thinking," Derek said as he slipped his hand around my waist. "You're thinking, *How the hell did I get here?*"

I looked into my groom's smiling eyes. "It's surreal, isn't it? How life can just change in an instant? You, my love, are a miracle, one that I never dreamed would happen. I was so done after Doug died. Completely resigned, finished, stick-a-fork-in-me done. But then you stepped on my foot—"

"And screwed up your carefully laid plans."

"No, smart-ass, you taught me I could live again. Not just survive, but actually live. I am so grateful you found us."

Derek pulled me into his chest, and we stood silently on the deck while the activity buzzed around us.

Robyn tapped me on the shoulder. "The guests are going to arrive soon. I need you to follow me so no one will see you." She led us back to the reception room where the bridal party would soon gather for the walk down the aisle. I peeked through the curtains to watch the guests arrive. Erin and Jon Frankel made their way over the cobblestones to the outside patio. Erin had given birth to their first daughter, Ariella, nearly eight months earlier. LaChanze arrived on the arm of her handsome fiancé, Derek Fordjour. She'd marry her Derek a month later with her daughters and his son, Langston, leading the way down the aisle. My heart leapt when I saw Joe Gardner navigating Charlotte through the well-dressed throng, both smiling and looking elegant in their fine clothes. Soon a gathering crowd of men in tuxedos escorting women in lavenders, greens, and yellows arrived and started to fill the chairs. I marveled at the Seattle crew. Every woman was tall, skinny, pretty, and looked as if she could run a marathon. The men all possessed that West Coast casual air with ruggedly handsome features, thick, tousled hair, and wide shoulders. My neatly coiffed New York mob was decidedly outgunned. But the Best Outfit prize went to the incomparable Stuart Fraser—in honor of his family ancestry, he arrived in full Scottish formal attire complete with kilt, flashes, and sporran. I heard Howard's voice above the others. He was herding his kids toward the anteroom where Allison was waiting with the wedding party. I'd asked the Lutnicks, Gottliebs, and Weinbergs to bring their children to the ceremony. In addition to Benjamin Weinberg and Kyle Lutnick, Vicky's daughter, Kay, was one of Michael's closest friends. They were born within weeks of each other, and every Sunday morning during those early years, the husbands would take the kids to brunch while their wives enjoyed a rare quiet hour in bed with the *New York Times*. Just as Derek and I were supported by our friends, we wanted Michael and Julia to share this important moment with theirs.

·····

The guests filled the rows, and the wedding party began to line up behind the curtains at the top of the aisle. The ushers and bridesmaids held branches or sprigs of cymbidium orchids, which they would add to the chuppah before sitting down. I hugged my bridesmaids; I would never be able to thank them enough for carrying us to this happy day. Derek straightened Michael's tie, and Julia ran her fingers through the soft petals in the white wicker basket she was holding. I walked toward the back of the line, suddenly cold and nervous. It was happening. The opening strains of Joe Cocker's "Have a Little Faith in Me" filled the air, and Rabbi Davidson disappeared through the curtain. I looked at Derek, who was staring blankly as if in a trance at the empty space where the rabbi had just been.

"Derek," I whispered. "Are you okay?"

"Of course," he answered too quickly. "Here we go."

From a distance one might have thought Derek looked anxious, but I could see something else entirely. It wasn't nerves; he was overcome. His eyes were wet, and he held a ball of tissue wedged in his left hand. The ushers started down the aisle.

"Honey, are you going to make it through the ceremony? I thought *I* would be the gusher."

"I can't control it. I just hope Rabbi Davidson has enough Kleenex up there."

The bridesmaids walked through the curtain. The line was getting shorter, and I stroked Derek's arm. I was deeply moved by his unexpected vulnerability and touched that he'd let loose his feelings. But I also didn't want this onslaught of raw emotion to prevent him from fully enjoying what was about to come. This was Derek's moment. I didn't want him to miss it.

"Derek, listen to me. During rehearsal you were so serious and tightly wound. This is *your* wedding. It's supposed to be joyous. Your friends and family didn't fly all the way out here to watch some stiff get married." I playfully punched him in the arm. "They want their pal, DT. I want DT. Honey, make an entrance. Put on a show. Have fun with this. It's only going to happen once."

Derek looked at me, stunned, as if he'd just won the lottery. Then the smile appeared. A big, mischievous smile that told me my groom was back from the brink.

"You're sure about this?"

"Go get 'em, baby."

Joe Cocker's voice continued to ring through the speakers. When Derek's parents took their turn down the aisle, Derek stepped into place behind the curtain. He shooed away the two attendants with a confident wave and took hold of the drapes in each hand. The music stopped, and Frank Sinatra's "The Best Is Yet to Come" began to play. At the moment Frank sings, "Out of the tree of life, I just picked me a plum," Derek tossed back the curtain and burst into the room like Johnny Carson on the *Tonight* show. Of course, I couldn't see Derek's antics, but I learned later that he did a little soft-shoe dance down the aisle, stopping here and there to greet guests and high-five his nephew. From my vantage point, however, all I could hear was wild laughter and mad applause. It was the most beautiful sound I'd ever heard.

When the laughter finally quelled, Michael and Julia started their stroll. Julia took her flower-girl job seriously and carefully scattered petals every two steps. My mother told me that Michael held fast to Julia's arm to keep her moving toward Derek. She also told me that Derek tearfully gathered the kids in a big bear hug under the chuppah, reached his hand into Julia's basket, grabbed the remaining petals, and flung them into the air, covering his delighted new daughter in a cascade of pink and white. I suspect Derek's greatest joy that day came from his realizing his new status as Michael and Julia's father. In a year, the four of us would appear before a Surrogate Court judge to finalize Derek's formal adoption of the kids. Derek told me that he wanted to commit to them, not just to their mother. He didn't want to change their names or replace Doug; he just wanted them to be his. "Marriages can end," he said. "But I want Michael and Julia to know I'll be theirs forever."

I listened to the happy gasps and tender clapping from my quiet position behind the curtain. I was alone now, standing silently in my white dress clutching three large calla lilies wrapped in a white satin ribbon. Ten years earlier, my father walked me down the aisle at the Essex House, the blue floral rug obscured under a white runner and rows of upholstered chairs. My veil caught on my eyelashes as we made our way past the dogwood candelabra to the wedding canopy. Doug stepped into the aisle and hugged my father. I could barely see through the veil and clung tightly to my bouquet. Doug's piercing blue eyes found mine, and he extended his hand. "Come with me," he whispered with a smile, knowingly repeating the words that changed my life that snowy January night.

And now, my life was changing again. I waited for the expected wave of fear and sadness to rush over me, but nothing happened. My heart beat steadily and, surprisingly, not a tear struck my eye. Finally, I knew with clarity that I was exactly where I was supposed to be. I belonged with Derek. Of course, I would never stop missing Doug; his unfathomable loss would always sting— closure is a myth. But Derek was not a consolation prize. He was the brass ring. He deserved to be loved fully, without restraint. And so did I.

Waiting for my cue, I was fully present, excited to walk down the aisle and see my dashing groom smile through his tears. He needed us as much as my kids and I needed him. If we could just live in the gray, somehow joy would find us.

For the last time, the music quieted, and my song, Fleetwood Mac's "Songbird," started to play.

For you, there'll be no more crying
For you, the sun will be shining
And I feel that when I'm with you,
It's alright, I know it's right.

The attendants held the curtain and waited for my cue. I took a deep breath and nodded. The fabric parted, and the room turned in unison.

Doug, come with me.

Acknowledgments

"Life isn't a matter of milestones,
but of moments."

—ROSE KENNEDY

First and foremost, *Where You Left Me* belongs to my husband,
Derek, and our magnificent children, Michael and Julia. Their
encouragement, humor, and patience were my salvation during
the writing process, which was often arduous and emotional. I
am forever indebted to my parents, Linda and Edward Radding,
my sister, Jayme Feldman, and her husband, Scott Feldman, for
their courage, strength, and a lifetime of love.

Thank you to Jennifer Bergstrom and Gallery Books/Simon
& Schuster for taking a chance on an unfinished manuscript by a
first-time writer. I am most grateful to Tricia Boczkowski, my edi-
tor, for her enthusiasm, incisive editorial input, and commitment
to this project. Added thanks also to Kate Dresser and Kristin
Dwyer.

There are many on whom I've depended during the writing of this book, but none more than the brilliant Abigail Pogrebin. She convinced me to put pen to paper, and her unwavering support and honest critiques have helped shape these pages. I'm also grateful to David Kuhn, my agent, for his excellent counsel and for ensuring that this book landed in the right hands every step of the way. Special thanks to Jessi Cimafonte and Billy Kingsland at Kuhn Projects for their invaluable assistance.

Allison and Howard Lutnick's constancy and optimism have carried me great distances, and our priceless friendship is one of the great blessings in my life. Their thoughtful comments on early drafts helped me reconstruct many of the stories in this book.

Pamela Weinberg and Vicky Gottlieb, my intrepid confidantes, have sustained me with stunning loyalty, wit, and compassion. Their detailed recollections and wise commentary were essential, and I thank them for showing me the humor even in the darker moments.

Joe and Charlotte Gardner's brave resolve to live fully and be our tender champions following the devastating loss of their adored son was nothing short of heroic. We greatly miss their spirited presence, and I hope that this book pays some tribute to their memories.

I was also inspired, critiqued and lovingly nudged along the way by Amy Koppelman, Elise and Stuart Fraser, LaChanze Fordjour, Erin Richards Frankel, Robin Shanus, Stephen Merkel, Edie Lutnick, Matthew Weinberg, David Gottlieb, Lynn Burkes, Rabbi Joy Levitt, Lori Schneider, Jodi Misher Peiken, Benjamin Weinberg, Kay Gottlieb, Kyle, Brandon and Casey Lutnick, and the Trulsons (Steven, Kristine, Amy, Jennifer, David, Samantha, Sevren and Kate).

With deep sadness and respect I remember the 658 employees of Cantor Fitzgerald who perished in the attacks on September 11, 2001. It will never matter how much time passes; the ache of their loss never dissipates. I think constantly of the victims of 9/11 and the families they left behind. In addition, I must acknowledge the firefighters, police officers, and rescue workers who risked and lost their lives to save others, and to everyone who worked at Ground Zero tirelessly—and at great physical peril—in the days, weeks, and months following the attacks. Their sacrifices were overwhelming and set a proud standard for our nation.

Finally, I thank my beautiful Douglas for every minute of the brief time we had together. You brought out the best in everyone you knew, and your noble example continues to inspire. You are my hero, always.

Douglas B. Gardner Foundation

The Douglas B. Gardner Foundation's mission is to support out-standing local organizations that provide valuable after-school programs for children who might otherwise fall through the cracks. Such programs typically offer opportunities for leadership and personal growth, provide mentoring and academic support, encourage children to be active participants in their own development, and engage them in fun and challenging activities.

Doug never took his good fortune for granted and giving back to the community was a priority. He served on the boards of several children's charities and talked of becoming an "angel" to a select group of motivated organizations that made a real difference in the lives of the kids they touched. Established in 2004, the Douglas B. Gardner Foundation will ensure that Doug will always be that angel; that in his name at-risk children will receive real support and opportunities to achieve success.

A portion of the author's proceeds from this book will be donated to the Douglas B. Gardner Foundation. To learn more visit www.dbgfoundation.org.